Enchantment of America

Hills and Harbors

THE MIDDLE ATLANTIC STATES

Delaware • Maryland • New Jersey • New York • Pennsylvania
West Virginia • District of Columbia

By Dorothy Wood

Illustrated by Vernon McKissack

CHILDRENS PRESS • CHICAGO

Educational Consultant for the
Enchantment of America Series:
Marilyn M. Spore, Laboratory School,
University of Chicago

Regional Consultant for

HILLS AND HARBORS:
Norman Carls, Ph.D.,
Adjunct Professor of Geography,
University of Pittsburgh

Library of Congress Catalog Card Number: 62-9073
Copyright, 1962, Childrens Press
Printed in the U.S.A.

Contents

The Land—then and now

Location

Great cities rubbing shoulders with fine farms—world seaports a few hours' drive from forest-clad mountains—ocean beaches and wide rivers—ridges and valleys and big lakes; these are some of the things that make up America's Middle Atlantic region. The states in this region are New York, Pennsylvania, New Jersey, Delaware, Maryland, and West Virginia. Washington, D. C., Capital of the United States, is here, too.

Formation and Change

Hundreds of millions of years ago, this land was covered by shallow seas. Time and time again, the land sank a little, and water flowed in from the sea to cover it. Then the land rose again, pushing the sea back. Each time this happened, a new layer of mud and sand lay where the water had been. Slowly, the layers built up, one on top of another.

In the layers of mud and sand were the bodies of countless sea animals, and from the different layers today we take the fossils of those animals—sponges, jellyfish, coral, sea stars, snails, clams, trilobites and crinoids of many kinds, fish, and many others.

Between floodings, many kinds of plants grew on the land. Plants grew, also, in the vast swamps where water stood in the lowlands. In the great forests of that early time grew tremendous club mosses like trees, horsetails as big as giant bamboo trees, and gigantic ferns. Animals crept through these forests—spiders, ancient scorpions, frogs, snails, and huge dragon flies. Some of the dragon flies measured two and a half feet from wing tip to wing tip.

The bodies of millions of these living things, plants and animals alike, became part of the layers that were building up. Water flooded the thick swamp forests and buried them under mud and sand and gravel. More layers spread over them, again and again.

All this material building up pressed down harder and harder on the layers beneath. These layers slowly changed to rock. Sandy layers became sandstone. The shells of sea animals were crushed together and became limestone. Gravel layers became conglomerate.

The swampy forest layers became coal. So great were the coal-making forests in this region that a large proportion of the world's coal has come from them. The Pittsburgh coal seam alone spreads under 20,000 square miles in western Pennsylvania, Ohio, and West Virginia. A much smaller area, some 500 square miles in northeastern Pennsylvania, was under greater pressure and made anthracite or "hard" coal. From this field comes most of the hard coal mined in America.

As the buried bodies of plants and animals decayed, petroleum was produced. Pennsylvania was the first state to recover this oil in quantity, and today is still a source of petroleum, along with neighboring areas in New York and West Virginia.

The increasing pressure began to push up the mountain ranges of the Appalachian system. Some of the rocks in the east were pressed together with such force and such heat that they melted and ran together. These became hard igneous rocks. The great pressure in that eastern area changed other rocks into hard metamorphic rocks. More pressure pushed these hard rocks up into rugged mountains. Water and wind began to wear away their softer parts. The Blue Ridge that remains today is only the hard stubs of these early, much higher mountain chains.

West of the Blue Ridge other folds of rock were pushed up. These were softer, sedimentary rocks, not melted together but squeezed until they had become limestone and sandstone. These rock folds were pushed hard from the southeast, and so made many rows of ridges, running from the northeast to the southwest. These make up today's ridge and valley country, the Folded Appalachians.

Farther west the valleys were filled in by erosion. In this far-flung area an almost level plateau formed, called the Allegheny or the Appalachian Plateau. Then the plateau rose a little through the central portion. So east of this central part, rivers ran to the east, and west of it, rivers ran to the west.

Here, erosion worked in two directions. A river might travel east down the sloping plateau, cutting a path across it. The river would cut across the tops of the old buried ridges, and keep on cutting down through them. Meanwhile, erosion from wind and rain was wearing away the softer earth between the old ridges, making valleys between them. So today rivers cut across some of the valleys and ridges, instead of running parallel to them. The Delaware River does this for part of its length. It cuts through the Kittatinny Mountains between New Jersey and Pennsylvania, making the famous "Delaware Water Gap." Similar gaps are cut by the Lehigh, Susquehanna, and Potomac rivers.

Never again, after the Appalachian system was lifted, did the seas come up and cover this part of the land as they had been doing over millions of years. But during the Ice Age some of the land was covered with ice. This began over a million years ago, and ended 10,000 to 12,000 years ago. Four or more times great ice sheets moved down over North America. They reached into New York, northern New Jersey and the northern corner of Pennsylvania. In western Pennsylvania they reached what is now the Ohio River.

Great ice sheets scoured the land and, melting, dropped their load of soil and gravel across river valleys, blocking them with high ridges, or moraines. So big lakes resulted—Lakes Erie and Ontario and the other Great Lakes, and many smaller ones in New York like the Finger Lakes, where long fingers of ice clawed at the land. The many deep ravines, or "glens," around the Finger Lakes today were dug out by moving ice and by rivers that formed when the ice melted.

With only the interruption of the advancing ice, living things came to the Middle Atlantic region. Fish swam in the sea, and the ancestors of the amphibians crept onto the land, followed by the first reptiles and the first birds. Dinosaurs roamed the marshy bottomlands and left many footprints, which we find today as fossils; mysteriously, few skeletons are found in this area. Then the dinosaurs died out, and mammals developed—small mammals like rats and mice at first, then larger and larger odd-appearing creatures with thick legs. Finally came the gigantic mammoths and mastodons. They were here when the ice came, and moved southward away from it. Along with many mammals that we know today were a great many that are gone now—huge bears and cats, giant ground sloths, and beavers as big as bears.

The Lay of the Land Today

When you think of the land in the Middle Atlantic country, there are three things to keep in mind: lakes, mountains, and seashore.

Two of the Great Lakes lie to the north, Lake Erie and Lake Ontario. Pennsylvania has a small frontage on Lake Erie; New York fronts along a section of the southeast shore of Lake Erie, and extends almost all the way along the southern shore of Lake Ontario. So these two states have a considerable lake plain, where rich soils were deposited by Ice-Age glaciers. The plains land is more or less level, but is broken here and there by low hills of loam, sand, clay, and gravel, dropped by melting ice. Glaciers formed many lakes in central and northern New York—the Finger Lakes, Lake Oneida, Lakes George and Champlain, and hundreds of others in the northern half of the state. Northern New Jersey, too, has many lakes made by glaciers.

Northern New York has a small offshoot of the Canadian Shield. The shield is a vast plateau, sometimes called the Laurentian Plateau, made up of very ancient high rock that has been changed little by upheaval, but was scoured by the ice sheets. It lies almost wholly in Canada, but dips into some of the states in the Middlewest, and into New York as well, where it forms nearly a perfect circle. The Adirondack Mountains of New York and the lovely lakes of the north are part of it.

Southeast of the Canadian Shield area the Appalachian Mountains rise, running from northeast to southwest, all the way from Nova Scotia to Alabama. In the north they are broken by the great St. Lawrence Valley. They are interrupted by other valleys, too. The Great Appalachian Valley runs north and south and takes in Lake Champlain and the Hudson. The Mohawk Valley reaches from the west and makes a wide lowland through the center of New York state—a route to the west much traveled by Indians and pioneering white men.

14

The Appalachians spread through Pennsylvania and West Virginia and the western "panhandle" of Maryland. Along their eastern front, the Blue Ridge runs through Maryland into Pennsylvania. West of there, with the Great Appalachian Valley between, the Folded Appalachians and the Allegheny Front take over, never more rugged than in West Virginia. Still farther west are the hills and myriad valleys of the Allegheny Plateau, where streams seem to run in almost all directions.

Wherever the rivers run, they cut through mountains and, dropping fast, make waterfalls. Niagara Falls, queen of all America's waterfalls, are formed where the Niagara River drops over the face of cliffs between Lakes Erie and Ontario. There are many other waterfalls, some of them hundreds of feet high, where the rivers have cut their way in all directions through the mountains to reach the Great Lakes, or the Ohio River, or the Atlantic Ocean.

East of the mountains, in southeastern Pennsylvania and in northern New Jersey and Delaware, is a little of the Piedmont, a region that covers much of the Atlantic states farther south. The Piedmont is an area where the softer parts of old mountains have been washed away, leaving a hill-and-valley country that jumps off quite suddenly, at the Fall Line, into the Atlantic Coastal Plain. Long Island in New York and much of New Jersey, Delaware, and eastern Maryland are made up of the Coastal Plain.

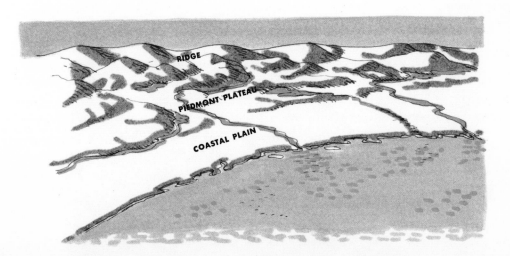

The Atlantic Coast all the way north and south through these states is a "drowned" shoreline. In ancient times, rivers like the Delaware, the Potomac, and the Susquehanna cut their way through the ridges and down through the Piedmont and the soft Coastal Plain, to make deep, wide channels where they met the sea. From the north, the Hudson River cut southward along the face of gigantic cliffs now called the Palisades, and, slicing through the Coastal Plain between Long Island and Staten Island, emptied into the Atlantic. Big and little tributaries flowed into these rivers; sometimes large branches met in tremendous mouths at the ocean's edge.

Then the land sank a little, and the sea rushed in. It poured into the mouths of the rivers, flooding or "drowning" them, and formed such tremendous bodies of water as Delaware and Chesapeake bays. These bays slash their way a hundred or two hundred miles inland. Chesapeake Bay almost divides Maryland in two; Delaware Bay separates Delaware from New Jersey; and the wide, wide mouth of the Potomac River separates Maryland from most of Virginia. At the mouth of the Hudson, the drowned river became New York Bay. The East River north of Long Island became Long Island Sound.

In all of these bodies of water, the old river channels are deep pathways for ocean-going ships.

As the sea water traveled into the many tributaries, winding shorelines formed in the bays. Then barrier islands built up in the ocean beyond them, formed by silt and sand carried by the ocean currents. Today nearly the whole coastline is protected by a thin line of these islands.

A famous coastline island is Long Island in New York. When the ice sheet moved down the Atlantic Coast, it stopped at Long Island, melted there, and moved no further south. The ice sheet dropped a hilly moraine on the north side of the island, which is today an area of low hills. From here the soft silt of the glacier washed down over the south side of the island, and so today this silty surface slopes off southward into the sea and makes the fine, sandy beaches of Long Island's southern shore.

Climate

Along with the many kinds of land in the Middle Atlantic States, there are many kinds of climate. In the north, and southward through the mountains, there are long, cold winters with deep snow. Temperatures often drop below zero. Summers are short and cool in the mountains throughout the region, but in the flatter areas of New York and in the valleys of New York and Pennsylvania, summers are likely to be as hot as the winters are cold. These lowland regions have a "continental" climate. In the areas close to the sea and near the big lakes, breezes from the water help to cool the land. Yet in New York City and in many other areas of the region, people often suffer through day after day of a summer heat wave, or blizzard after blizzard of a winter storm, with subzero temperatures.

Off the shores of New Jersey, Delaware, and Maryland flows the ocean's warm Gulf Stream. When winds blow from the Gulf Stream they help to warm the land in winter. So the coastal regions enjoy periods of mild weather in winter as well as pleasant summers cooled by ocean breezes.

All of the Middle Atlantic States have an abundance of rainfall. Combined with the warm summer sunshine of the level and valley areas, which have a fairly long growing season, this makes for wonderful growing conditions for crops and gardens. Some of the finest farms and gardens in the world are here.

Things to think about

What part did water and living things play in the formation of the Middle Atlantic lands?

How were the mountains, ridges, plateaus and valleys of the region formed?

Why are there so many lakes and rivers in this region?

How were the great bays and coastal islands formed?

Describe the general "lay of the land" today and the major land forms of the region.

What things affect the climate of the Middle Atlantic region?

People come to the middle atlantic

The First People

More than 25,000 years ago, scientists think, the first people came to North America. Ice in the great sheets of the Ice Age still covered the northern part of the land, leaving some of Alaska free, but reaching down into the country where the Great Lakes are today. The sea level was lower than it is now, and probably a land pathway extended across Bering Strait. Or perhaps there was an ice bridge across the strait.

Along this pathway, perhaps on land, perhaps on ice, people came to North America from Asia—small, brown people with straight, black hair and dark skins. They were the ancestors of the American Indian, and we call them, too, "Indians."

Probably they were hunters. Perhaps several men in a group, bringing their families along, followed the big game of the Ice Age. Huge mammoths and elephants, giant bears, ground sloths, saber-toothed tigers, camels and horses were some of the animals pushed southward by the ice. The hunters had only spears, with sharp, beautifully fluted spear points of stone. But hunting together, they could kill the big animals, and they followed them southward and spread far and wide over the American continent.

Many of them went into the Southwest, many into the Southeast. Still others followed the Mississippi Valley. Some reached the Middle Atlantic region and hunted through what is now New York and Pennsylvania.

The Algonquians

For thousands of years these Middle Atlantic Indians led a simple, peaceful life. They hunted in scattered groups, and these separated groups developed into tribes. They spoke languages that came to be so different that they could not understand each other. But the languages were related, just as the French and English languages of today are related. All these tribes belonged to one language stock or "family," the Algonquian.

The tribes that spoke Algonquian languages belonged to the great group of Eastern Woodlands Indians. Some other language families belonged to this group, too, because the Indians that spoke these other languages lived somewhat like the Algonquian-speaking tribes.

The Algonquians lived in pleasant valleys, such as the Mohawk Valley in New York, and in the lake plains of New York and Pennsylvania. They lived near the Atlantic shores, where living was easier than in the mountains. But while they farmed in the lowlands and fished in the ocean and lakes and streams, they made hunting trails through the mountains, too.

Where there were birch trees, they used the bark to make canoes, so wonderfully light in weight that they could be carried from one stream to another. If birch bark was not available, elm bark was used, which made heavier but still serviceable canoes. So transportation on water was theirs—on the water of the bays and the large river mouths and the lakes.

They used bark, too, for their houses, thatching their wigwams with it or with woven mats. The wigwams were rounded huts, made with thatch laid over a framework of bent poles. Since the Indians hunted, these homes were never permanent. They could not be taken up and carried along, but they were so simple that they could be built quickly on a new spot. When game ran out, the Indians simply abandoned their homes, moved to a new place, and built new wigwams.

Their clothing in wintertime, in this land of snow and ice, had to be warm. Men and women alike wore buckskin leggings. Over them the women wore fringed buckskin dresses reaching below their knees, and the men wore fringed shirts and kilts, or short skirts. They used snowshoes made of wooden frames and a webbing of sinews to walk across the snow.

In spite of the hard winters and their halfway nomadic life of the hunter, these Indians were good farmers. Many of their possessions show that they traded with tribes from the Southeast. In that way, corn came to them. The Algonquians raised corn all the way through the Middle Atlantic region, along with squash, pumpkins, and potatoes. They planted beans and corn together and cooked them together, in a dish that we cook today and for which we still use the Indian name— succotash. They made maple sugar from the sap of the maple trees, cooking it down and letting it harden in vats of birch bark.

The Indians made a crude kind of pottery and did simple weaving, which they traded back and forth with Indians of other areas. Their tools were made from stone or hard wood, for they still had not learned the use of metals.

The Algonquians were probably in contact with the Mound Builders, to the south and to the west. In fact these highly civilized Indians, who built mounds all up and down the valleys of the Mississippi and Ohio rivers, built one of the largest of them at Moundsville, in West Virginia, near where Grave Creek empties into the Ohio River. Today in the town of Moundsville you can see this big burial ground, one of the most famous built by the prehistoric peoples. The Middle-Atlantic Algonquian tribes undoubtedly traded with the Mound Builders, and perhaps learned farming from them.

The Iroquois Move North

Another group of Woodlands Indians had developed in the region between the Algonquians and the Cherokees of Georgia and Alabama. These were the Iroquoians, related to the Cherokees but different enough to make a language family of their own. Long before the white men came to the Middle Atlantic region, the Iroquoians had spread northward through Ohio, Pennsylvania, New York, and into Canada. They were fighters, and strongly organized. They were able to raid and defeat the Algonquians. They pushed them in two directions, toward the seacoast and toward the Middlewest.

The Iroquoians lived in the famous "long houses," a whole clan of several families in one "long house." The houses made up a village, around which the Iroquois often built a strong stockade. As were all the other Woodlands Indians, they were hunters and fishermen, and they farmed, too, to supplement the game they killed.

In these simple surroundings the Woodlands Indians lived, slept, and raised their families. They had a strong religion, based on the happenings of nature around them—the change of seasons, in which the god of life defeated the ice god—the changes from morning to night, the stars, the events in the lives of animals, and all the other happenings close to these people who lived mostly out-of-doors. Their foods were gifts of the gods, and so the first food in a season was frequently offered to a special god. The Iroquois' Society of Faces, in which the wearers of hideous masks were thought to be able to control diseases, still exists today in the New York reservations. And these Indians, like many others, never strike a child, to punish him, but threaten him with a masked goblin, "Long Nose," who might carry him away.

When the white man settled in the Middle Atlantic region, there were five strong Iroquois tribes in New York and Pennsylvania, between the Hudson and Ohio rivers. They were the Mohawk, the Oneida, the Onandaga, the Cayuga, and the Seneca. They were banded together in a league that we call "The Five Nations."

25

Explorers from Europe

Long before Captain John Smith and his English colonists came to Jamestown, the French had been fishing up and down the Atlantic Coast, and had been sailing into such harbors as Chesapeake Bay to trade for furs with the Indians. Then, in 1609, several things happened.

Champlain, the French explorer, moved into New York, coming southward along the lake that now bears his name. He not only explored the area, but gave his help to the Algonquian Indians against their Iroquois enemies.

Henry Hudson, an Englishman working for the Dutch Republic, sailed into the giant harbor at the mouth of the Hudson River, and Delaware Bay as well, and claimed them for the Netherlands.

Captain Smith ranged north of the Jamestown settlement and explored and charted Chesapeake Bay.

Colonies in the New World

So there were three European countries making strong bids for colonies in this part of the New World. Strongest, at first were the Dutch. Dutch trading posts and settlements sprang up along the Hudson in what are now the states of New York and New Jersey. In the center of their "New Netherland" the Dutch established a strong settlement on Manhattan Island, called *New Amsterdam*. They settled along the Delaware River also, in New Jersey and Pennsylvania, where Philadelphia now stands and along Delaware Bay in New Jersey and Delaware. When Sweden, too, sent colonists to the area, the Dutch took over the Swedish settlements.

New Netherland came to be a great center, in the very heart of the rich Middle Atlantic region. The Dutch enjoyed a rich fur trade with the Indians, and, befriending the Iroquois, traded them guns to use against their Algonquian and French enemies.

Then the Dutch went to war with England, and lost the war. All the Dutch colonies in America went to the English. New Netherland became the province of New York, and New Amsterdam became New York City.

The English, too, were friends of the Iroquois, and helped them in their fight against the French and the Algonquian tribes. South from New York Harbor, William Penn had been given a great grant of land that took in most of Pennsylvania; later he acquired Delaware also. He dealt fairly with the Delaware Indians, an Algonquian tribe, and through his lifetime the settlers had no trouble with them. But later the whites advanced onto Delaware lands, and the Indians turned against them. So even this friendly tie with the Algonquian tribes was broken.

Still farther south was the Maryland area, almost surrounding the vast Chesapeake Bay. This area was chartered by the English crown in 1632, and two years later Lord Baltimore established the colony of St. Mary's City. Here was a strong English colony, although it was often raided by Algonquian Indians who wanted to keep open the pathway of their fur trade with the French.

Many of the colonists were living for the first time in comparative freedom. They came from war-torn lands where they had been told how they could and could not worship, where their governing was done for them, where they had been denied the right to own property. Many of them worked for years as indentured servants for someone who paid their passage to the New World. When free at last of that debt, they were also free to buy land, and, owning property, they could vote.

These people had earned the right to govern themselves, and they prized this right highly, as part of the personal freedom offered by their new country. Each colony had its representative house with members elected by the people, as well as a council or house and a governor appointed by the king or by the proprietor of the colony. These groups were responsible for making laws for the colonies.

Churches in the Middle Atlantic colonies were separate from the governing bodies. Yet attending church was a most important way in which the people of the times kept up with what was going on in their country. Each week they came from miles around to go to church, and after the services they visited with each other, exchanging news and opinions, and deciding what course or what man could best serve the community.

28

For the most part, the Middle Atlantic colonists were farmers and people living in small trading towns and villages. In the Tidewater of Maryland, where tobacco was grown, there were big plantations. The plantation was the center of the community, with boats coming to its docks to bring goods and take away tobacco. The wealthy plantation owner lived in a fine mansion and kept Negro slaves to care for it and for his tobacco fields.

But farther north and west, all through the river valleys, small farms were the heart of the land where each family made its own way by growing wheat, corn, hay, potatoes, and other crops, and raising livestock. These people were not wealthy enough to hire help. Instead, the members of each family worked together, to provide food and shelter and some crops to sell, and to provide most of the things of daily living. They spun thread and wove cloth for clothing and household items, and made tools and furniture and dishes. If they had an excess of anything, they took it to the nearest village and traded it for something they could not make.

This was only the beginning of a trade that went on briskly with the other American colonies up and down the Atlantic Coast, and with countries overseas. The deep forests spread over the land provided wood of many kinds. Small sawmills sprang up along the streams to cut the wood into lumber for shipping abroad. Ships were often made of American wood, and were often built in the new American harbor cities like New York and Philadelphia. Iron was mined throughout the Middle Atlantic colonies and the ore was shipped away or used in America to manufacture iron tools and equipment.

From the West, beyond the farms and the sawmills, came furs, traded by the Indians to the white men for beads, knives, and other articles of metal, and for guns and whiskey.

England and France Fight for Fur Trade

Fur trading, in fact, was a main point of the struggle between the French and the English for control of this continent. The Algonquian tribes lined up with the French and the Iroquois lined up with the English. The struggle was called the French and Indian War, lasting from 1754 to 1763. In this war George Washington of Virginia and many other early American heroes received important training and experience.

Pennsylvania and New York, in the center of the most heavily populated and coveted region, saw some of the heaviest of the fighting. The Ohio Valley was a major route into the West from both the French colonies to the north and those of the English to the east. Fort Duquesne was built by the French after they defeated English settlers. Fort Duquesne stood at the head of the Ohio, at the junction of the Monongahela and Allegheny rivers, where Pittsburgh now stands, and controlled the Ohio Valley. An English attempt to recapture the fort from the French resulted in the famous Braddock defeat and in General Braddock's death. But later in the war, the fort was taken by British troops. Other important battles were fought in New York, especially on Lake George and Lake Champlain, at Fort Ticonderoga and Crown Point.

The English won this war, too, and the French hold on the North American continent was broken.

The Revolutionary War

The English were not to continue long as masters. The Americans were now strong enough to fight for what they wanted, and they wanted liberty and self-government. They had learned to take care of themselves, to provide their own food and shelter, even to do their own governing.

Again the Middle Atlantic region was in the midst of the struggle, this time a struggle for independence. Philadelphia was the colonies' most important meeting center. The First and Second Continental Congresses met there, and the Declaration of Independence was signed there, in Independence Hall. Of the 56 signers, 25 were from the Middle Atlantic colonies. A prominent Philadelphian, Benjamin Franklin, was one of the most active leaders in Revolutionary times; Alexander Hamilton of New York was another.

Many of the important battles of the Revolution centered around the big harbors, where the English fleet could unload their armies. Early in the war, General Washington fought for and lost Long Island and New York harbor. These important locations remained in British hands until the end of the war.

Washington, retreating from New York, crossed New Jersey with the British at his heels and put the Delaware River between the two armies. Then, from the Pennsylvania side, he crossed the river on a bitter Christmas night to attack Britain's hired Hessian troops and to defeat the British at Trenton. General Washington and his troops went on to win the battle of Princeton and drive the English out of New Jersey.

But the British struck at Pennsylvania and were successful in occupying Philadelphia, with bitter defeats to the Americans on the Brandywine River and at Germantown. Washington withdrew to Valley Forge, a few miles west of Philadelphia, and spent the worst winter of the war.

Yet even before Valley Forge, the British had begun to lose the war. They had laid plans to subdue New England and northern New York by sending an army under General Burgoyne, from Canada down the Hudson River, to join an army moving north from New York City. But the army from New York City was slow in starting, and General Burgoyne was defeated and surrendered his army at Saratoga.

This defeat had another important effect besides keeping the north free. For a long time France had been friendly to the colonies. Lafayette, the brilliant young Frenchman, was one of Washington's generals and most trusted friends. Lafayette served with valor and spent the terrible Valley Forge winter with Washington. Benjamin Franklin had been working to persuade France to join the colonies in the war, but France was reluctant to move in the face of British victories. After Saratoga, however, it looked as if the Americans might have a chance. So France came into the war on the side of the colonies, and sent them an army and a fleet.

Months stretched into years as these things happened, and it was fours years after Saratoga before the last campaign ended. The British, after their defeat in the north, felt the south to be a softer field of attack and sent Lord Cornwallis with an army into the southern colonies. He captured Savannah, Georgia, and moved northward, all the way to Yorktown, Virginia, where he sent to New York for reinforcements and a fleet to take over Chesapeake Bay. But there he was finished. Washington quickly brought the combined American and French army to bottle him up in Yorktown, and the French fleet sailed into the bay and kept his ships from bringing help. In October, 1781, Cornwallis surrendered, and the war was over.

The Young Nation

All of the Middle Atlantic States except West Virginia, which was then part of Virginia, were among the original thirteen of the United States. Delaware was the first to ratify the Constitution, Pennsylvania was second, and by 1788 all five Middle Atlantic States had ratified.

Philadelphia and, later, New York City took leading positions in the nation as centers of commerce and finance. World ports grew up in these cities and at such other natural harbors as Wilmington, Delaware, and Baltimore, Maryland. From 1785 to 1790, New York City was the young nation's capital. There George Washington was inaugurated as the first President of the United States. But there was rivalry between the North and South for the capital's location, and it was moved to Philadelphia in 1790, where it remained for ten important years. But still the location argument was not settled. So, on land that Maryland and Virginia had given, the District of Columbia was established. In 1800 the capital was moved to Washington, D.C., and there Thomas Jefferson was inaugurated as the third President of the United States.

Through these years people were pouring into the new country from Europe. Cities grew larger as their industries grew. Indians in the eastern part of the region were a thing of the past. Many of the Algonquian tribes were wiped out by disease and the wars, and those that survived moved into Canada to avoid their Iroquois enemies to the west.

But in the west, there was still trouble with the Iroquois. They had sided with the British during the Revolutionary War and had raided frontier settlements. After the war, the raiding went on. Finally the United States sent troops up the Mohawk River, and the power of the Iroquois was broken. They were moved to reservations in New York, and still live on them today.

A Way to Travel

Now the western areas of New York and Pennsylvania were open to settlement, and people traveled up the Mohawk and the Allegheny rivers and settled in the valleys. There was a great need for better transportation. The mountains were full of coal and other minerals, and the valleys had plentiful farm crops. But products are without value unless they can be moved to places where people can use them, and so the western interior needed to move its products to the big-city markets of the east. It needed a way to bring more people there for settlement. Those people needed goods from the eastern factories.

The National Road, built from Cumberland in western Maryland to what is now Wheeling, West Virginia, was important. It reached the Ohio River and went on toward St. Louis, ending near the Mississippi River. The Mohawk Trail through the Appalachians and up the Mohawk Valley enabled riders and wagons to reach central New York. But even so, most of New York was still a country apart. And beyond, reaching ever westward along the Ohio and across the Great Lakes and the Mississippi, lay the vast unsettled lands of the West. Here any improvement at all in transportation of people and goods meant important development in the settlement of this far-flung frontier.

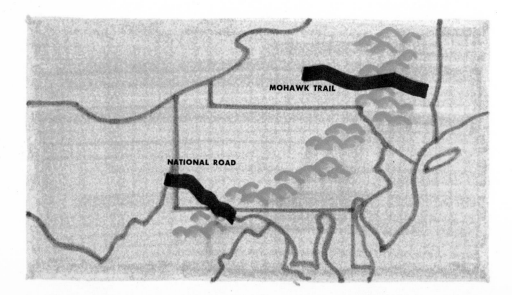

The Erie Canal

So there came to be one of the most ambitious undertakings in the history of our nation—the Erie Canal. Built at a time when there was no heavy machinery for earth moving, the canal was dug by hand. Horses and mules hauled the dirt away. The canal ran all the way from the Hudson River to Lake Erie. It provided transportation across the center of the state of New York, connecting the ports of the Great Lakes and the Atlantic Ocean. The canal boats were pulled by teams of horses or mules walking along the bank. Today a portion of the Erie Canal, dug deeper and wider, is a part of the New York State Barge Canal.

Soon after the canal was dug, men began building railroads. One of the first was the Baltimore and Ohio, running west from Maryland. Pennsylvania, too, was building canals, roads, and railroads. All up and down the seacoast, ships were being built in the big harbor cities.

Power for Industry

Coal was coming to the harbor cities from mines in the mountains, and to cities along the Ohio River. Iron ore from the Great Lakes region came to the port cities for the iron industries of Pennsylvania and the region that is now West Virginia. Then came oil, when the first successful oil well in the United States was drilled at Titusville, Pennsylvania. Both the supply of power and the importance of the region's industry took great leaps ahead.

With fuel and iron coming from the west, with people continuing to come from across the sea, and with great markets opening in the west as well as overseas, the eastern cities grew larger and larger. The destiny of the region was set as one of the greatest industrial areas that the world has ever known.

War Between the States

The Middle Atlantic States were often "in the middle" when it came to important happenings in this country. So it was with the War Between the States. The five original Middle Atlantic States all stayed with the Union. Even Maryland, where slaves were used on the Tidewater plantations, declared herself for the Union and against secession. This region was, in fact, a borderland between the North and the South, and as a borderland it had people who felt strongly on both sides of the conflict.

The part of Virginia along the Ohio River and in the northwestern mountains had developed very differently from the eastern part of the state where big plantations and coastal cities were common. The mountain region needed roads and other development for which eastern Virginia would not pay. The mountain and river people developed along entirely different lines, of thought and community life, from the plantation people and those of the eastern cities. When the state of Virginia seceded from the Union, the northwestern part, most of the river and mountain region, pulled away from that state and became West Virginia, joining the Union in 1863.

In that same year came one of the biggest battles in the war, at Gettysburg, Pennsylvania, where Abraham Lincoln later gave an address that became immortal. This was the farthest north of any battle in the war, and the Confederates' defeat there became the turning point of the war. In Maryland, too, there was fighting; that at Antietam was the most important.

After the War

The Middle Atlantic region had little of the painful reconstruction period that haunted the South. Recovery was quick, and the big cities soon were booming from the Ohio River to the seacoast. The iron and steel industries developed rapidly, and Pittsburgh became the queen of the nation's steel empire. Coal and more coal was mined in the mountains. Bituminous coal came easily from the great strip mines of western Pennsylvania and West Virginia. Anthracite coal came from deep underground in eastern Pennsylvania. Coal was the principal fuel that heated homes and ran factories and furnaces across the nation.

The city of New York grew by leaps and bounds, filling Manhattan Island and spilling over to Staten Island and Long Island and northward along the mainland. Early the business center of the nation, this city soon took political and cultural leadership as well. Here, almost before the war was over, was the greatest city in the world.

Things to think about

In what way did the climate, and the land and its resources influence the way the Algonquian Indians lived?

How were the Iroquoian Indians different from the Algonquians?

In what ways did England, the Netherlands and France influence the Middle Atlantic region?

What part did this region and its people play in the Revolutionary War?

How did new developments in transportation influence the growth of the Middle Atlantic States?

What effect did the Civil War have on the people, industries, and cities of the Middle Atlantic States?

Life in the middle atlantic states today

The Big Cities

New York is one of the biggest cities and greatest harbors in the world. In Greater New York are five big boroughs. Each one makes up part of the life of this fabulous harbor city; each one is entirely or nearly surrounded by water.

Manhattan Island, the borough of skyscrapers, has New York Bay south of it, the Hudson River on the west, the East River on the east, and the Harlem River on the east and north. Here is the heart of the city—Wall Street and the New York Stock Exchange—Rockefeller Center—Broadway and the Metropolitan Opera. Here is the Battery and much of the shipping of the complex harbor where an ocean liner is always at one dock or another. Here are hundreds of other features that make New York the commercial and cultural center of America. When the island filled and the city could not grow out in any direction, it grew up, and great skyscrapers formed its famous skyline.

The other boroughs are Staten Island, in the bay south of Manhattan; Brooklyn, east across the East River on Long Island; Queens, north of

Brooklyn; and The Bronx, on the mainland north of Queens and separated from it by the East River.

Within the city limits live eight million people, nearly half of the people in the whole state of New York. They live with the sea lapping at their very doors, and yet go their way in a maze of city streets and gigantic buildings, where bridges cross rivers and tunnels burrow underneath them. Automobiles and subway trains take people back and forth to work and home again from one water-bounded part of town to another. The east shore of New Jersey, along the Hudson, is reached the same way. Ferries chug back and forth from Staten Island. Also connecting the five boroughs is an incredible network of tubes and lines for sending mail, telephone service, electricity, gas, and water. Anything happening to the underground and underwater channels of any of these can paralyze large sections of the city for hours on end.

Mighty as it is, New York is not the whole story of eastern cities. West of New York and reaching south all the way to Washington, D.C., is an area built up so closely that small towns and cities merge into one another. Driving here, you are always near city streets built up with stores and shopping centers, housing developments, and factories. Almost the only "country" that these city dwellers see is in their parks.

Across the Hudson from New York, New Jersey's Newark and Jersey City share the great port facilities of the harbor and are manufacturing and transportation centers in their own right. Here water transportation changes to air, rail, and highway to cross the continent. Trenton stands at the head of navigation on the Delaware River. Camden is a big manufacturing and shipbuilding city and marine terminal farther down the river.

Across the Delaware in Pennsylvania, Philadelphia is another of the East's leading centers of manufacturing, shipping, finance, and culture. One of the large cities of the world, her seaport is second in this country only to New York. Oil, coal, and grain, iron and steel, metal products, textiles, and many other manufactured products travel all over the world from Philadelphia, often in ships of her own building.

Downriver, Wilmington, in Delaware, also has tremendous shipyards, as well as plants for building railroad equipment and great chemical-manufacturing plants. Baltimore, Maryland, is still another great port. Baltimore's outlets to the sea extend through the Chesapeake and Delaware Canal, leading to Delaware Bay, and through Chesapeake Bay. Baltimore is our nation's third busiest seaport, after New York and Philadelphia.

On still another river, the Potomac, is Washington, D.C., seat of the government of the United States. Here is a city planned to be the Capital. All its streets, parks, buildings, and other facilities are planned to take care of the hundreds of governmental offices and the people called to Washington by government business. The Capitol Building itself, on a hill overlooking the whole area, is the beautiful and impressive high point of this city.

On the Ohio River, Pittsburgh is in the center of Pennsylvania's vast bituminous coal fields. With coal at hand, and iron ore brought in from mines near Lake Superior and eastern Canada, Pittsburgh is the top-ranking iron and steel manufacturing center of the East. West Virginia's cities of Charleston, Huntington, and Wheeling are important producers of chemicals, glass, coal, and iron and steel.

Transportation and Communication

The St. Lawrence Seaway makes it possible for seagoing ships to go up the St. Lawrence River and into the Great Lakes. They travel the river along the northern boundary of New York and enter Lake Ontario. They go around Niagara Falls by way of the Welland Canal into Lake Erie and often stop at Buffalo, and so this city is another world port for New York state.

The seaway is only one of several waterways. South of New York City the Intracoastal Waterway takes care of much shipping along the coast, using the long water lanes protected by barrier islands. The New York State Barge Canal runs across the state from Buffalo and Oswego on Lakes Erie and Ontario to Troy on the Hudson River. Albany, near Troy, is at the head of navigation on the Hudson and so is reached by ocean-going ships. Farther south the Chesapeake and Delaware Canal handles water traffic between the heads of the two bays.

Water transportation, over water lanes used in early times by Indians and explorers, may be the most colorful part of this story, but it is also only the beginning.

The whole Middle Atlantic region is a network of fine highways—of limited access freeways and toll roads where vast numbers of cars whizz along north and south, east and west, through Pennsylvania, New York, New Jersey, and the other states of the region and beyond. Connecting with these are many fine highways into all parts of the states, so that both passenger and truck traffic can go quickly from one place to another. Railroads, too, are a network; and every state has huge airports. In the New York and Washington airports, foreign and domestic planes come and go every minute of the day.

The big cities, too, are centers of television and radio, sending out news announcements and entertainment programs to every corner of the Middle Atlantic region and the nation, and to many parts of the world. Telephoning has reached the stage where you can pick up your telephone and dial directly to a telephone across the continent.

Middle Atlantic Farm Lands

Even with all this fine transportation and communication, the cities could not easily exist without close-by farms. But the farms are there, in the rich soil of valleys and coastal plain alike. In most of the interior of New York, Pennsylvania, and West Virginia, the valleys big and little are filled with farms. New York is second in the United States in the production of milk, and produces so much cheese that one kind is named "New York." The chief farm crop, as in Pennsylvania, is hay to feed the dairy cattle; other important crops are oats, corn, wheat, barley, buckwheat, and many kinds of fruit—apples, grapes, peaches, pears, cherries, and others. Central and southern New Jersey's bogs produce quantities of cranberries and blueberries. Just as New York and Pennsylvania gave maple sap to the Indians, they give it now to their white citizens, in large quantities.

On the coastal plains of New Jersey, Long Island, Maryland and Delaware, truck gardening is the leading farming activity. Here are grown millions of tons of vegetables required by the people of the big cities—tomatoes, corn and beans, cabbages, cauliflower and broccoli, onions and celery. A far cry, these tremendous truck gardens, from the days when the Indians dropped four grains of corn and a couple of beans into each hill in their village gardens!

Natural Resources

Fertile soils and vast waters for transportation are not the only natural resources of this rich region. As we have seen, there is water power everywhere—waterfalls formed as the rivers rush from the highlands to reach the sea. Niagara alone is one of the world's greatest power producers, for manufacturing in dozens of nearby cities.

When you think of minerals in the Middle Atlantic, you think first of coal, especially in Pennsylvania and West Virginia and western Maryland; and then you think of oil and natural gas, found in New York as well. These states have other minerals—building stones like granite and sandstone and slate; rock from which cement is made; and clay that goes into bricks and fine pottery and porcelain. They and New Jersey mine zinc; bauxite comes from Maryland; New York is first in production of talc, supplies fine abrasive garnets and emery, and along with Pennsylvania and West Virginia mines much of the country's rock salt and salt brines, important in the manufacture of chemicals.

Forests and lumbering have a prominent place in the Middle Atlantic story. Nearly half of Pennsylvania, most of West Virginia and a third of New York are in forests. Spread over the mountains and across the Allegheny highlands are great stands of white pine, balsam, spruce, hemlock, maple and birch, in the north and in higher altitudes; in central and southern areas are oak, beech, hickory, walnut, and many others. Pine forests cover nearly half of New Jersey, including the Pine Barrens in the southern part of the state, once wholly cut over but now covered by second growth. Delaware and Maryland, too, have important stands of forest. Manufacture of paper and paper products and processing of lumber and other wood products are important activities in all the Middle Atlantic States.

What Pennsylvania is to coal, Maryland, Delaware, and New Jersey are to the fishing industry. No product is anywhere more famous than Maryland's Chesapeake Bay oysters, and Delaware and New Jersey both have large oyster beds in Delaware Bay. Clams and crabs are also taken in great numbers here, along with such fish as bass, trout, perch, alewives, and bluefish, and great quantities of menhaden for oil and fertilizer.

The People

Nowhere is the great "melting pot" of America more in evidence than in the Middle Atlantic States. This region was settled by English, Dutch, Swedes, and to some extent the French from the north and the Spanish from the south. The Irish came in the middle of the 1800's because of famine in their country, and stayed to build canals and railways and work in factories. People oppressed in Europe by poverty and politics came from every country to America, the Land of Opportunity.

Many of them stopped to work in the industries of the seaboard cities. New York's millions are in great measure the descendants of these immigrants, in their blood the stock of England, Scotland, Ireland, Germany, France, Italy, Hungary, Czechoslovakia, Poland, Lithuania, and many other nations.

The industries and commerce of the other great cities reflect these same people, many of them arriving at the beginning of this century, others at the time when America's first immigrants came to her shores. Some are even older in their ancestry; in New York are Indian reservations of the Senecas, and in Delaware are the "White Indians" who descended from the Nanticoke tribe that the first white explorers and settlers found there.

While workers poured into the country to man its growing industries, great fortunes were being amassed by some of those who owned the industries—people who made this the great financial region of the country. They were people like Andrew Carnegie, Andrew W. Mellon, and Charles M. Schwab who made fortunes in Pennsylvania steel and coal and headed great financial empires in New York and other cities; like John Wanamaker, who built his empire as a clothing merchant in New York City, and Frank W. Woolworth, who started the first Woolworth store in Pennsylvania and went on to erect the famous Woolworth Building in New York City; and like John D. Rockefeller, for whom is named a city within a city, Rockefeller Center, in the heart of New York.

Many of the people who work in the cities live away from the city, in suburbs or in the country. Hundreds of thousands travel each morning from New Jersey, for example, into New York City and into Philadelphia, and return to their homes in the evening. People live in Connecticut and go to work each day in Manhattan.

Farmers in the Middle Atlantic have the same great mixture of nationalities that are so characteristic of the cities. The Italians, especially, have made the region's truck gardens famous.

In the District of Columbia the city of Washington, which fills the District and spills over into Maryland and Virginia, determines the kind of people who live there. Hundreds of thousands of people go there because they are connected with the United States Government —people from all over America who have a part in Government or who work in the offices. Other thousands come from all over the world—diplomats who live in Washington from year to year and those who come for conferences of a few days or a few weeks.

The Arts

Cities like New York, Philadelphia, and Washington early made the Middle Atlantic the cultural center of America. New York, especially, took the lead and became the great magnet for writers, artists, architects, sculptors, musicians, and actors. Here was the greatest publishing center of the world, the art showplace, and Broadway, the "Great White Way," dazzling from its lights and from the brilliance of its theater. Here were ballet and opera and symphony; here was the "Tin Pan Alley" of jazz and popular music. What was true in New York was almost equally true in the other big cities of the region and in many not so big.

Hundreds of museums all over the region hold its cultural products as well as those from all over the country. In them you will find exhibits ranging from the creative crafts such as the glass-blowing and wood-carving of Pennsylvania and the needlecraft and pottery and weaving of West Virginia to New York City's most sophisticated modern paintings. The National Gallery of Art in Washington and the Metropolitan Museum of Art in New York City are two of the most famous art museums; there are many others, in almost any large town or city. Historical museums all over the area preserve the fine furniture and other antiques of a by-gone day.

Fine music, too, comes from this region—from the symphony orchestras of Philadelphia and New York and other cities; from Carnegie Hall; from the Metropolitan Opera, and from dozens of other sources. The Juilliard School of Music in New York is only one of the many fine schools that teach one or another branch of the arts.

Nowhere in our country is our great variety of architecture more apparent than in eastern cities. New York's Empire State Building rockets to 102 stories, and many others reach 60 and 70 stories. Some of the old manor houses in which early residents of the Middle Atlantic lived are still furnished just as they were in those days. Magnificent churches and great university buildings rub shoulders with early simple meeting houses, their straight, clean lines reminding us of the lives of our first settlers.

A list of the famous people in the arts of this region might go on for many pages. Benjamin Franklin was among the earliest, as publisher of the *Philadelphia Gazette* and author of *Poor Richard's Almanack*. Walt Whitman lived in New York, Washington, and New Jersey most of his life; Washington Irving and James Fenimore Cooper wrote about early New York. There were hundreds of others born in the region or who came here to work for a considerable part of their lives. They include writers Herman Melville, Horatio Alger, Edgar Allen Poe, Bret Harte, John Burroughs, Owen Wister, Christopher Morley, Clarence Day, and Eugene O'Neill; musicians Stephen Foster, Edward MacDowell, Walter Damrosch, Irving Berlin, and Leonard Bernstein; artists Benjamin West, Gilbert Stuart, George Inness, Frederic Remington, and George Catlin; and many, many others. Key Bridge in Washington is named after Francis Scott Key, author of our national anthem, whose home once stood on the banks of the Potomac near the site of the bridge.

Education and Research

Almost before the first settlers landed in the Middle Atlantic, they were thinking about schools. School was held in a little log cabin, or perhaps in someone's home, and the teacher was often someone working off a debt for his passage to America. Often he earned little cash, but was paid in room and board and crops from field and garden.

Private schools, where the parents of each child paid sometimes a large sum for his education, grew up from some of these. Others became free schools. Early in the colonies' history all of these states, or the counties in them, established free schools.

From these beginnings grew up some of the greatest educational institutions of America—schools like Princeton and Rutgers universities, in New Jersey, and Columbia and Cornell universities in New York. The United States Military Academy was early established at West Point, on the Hudson in New York. Annapolis, Maryland, is the home of the United States Naval Academy. Women's colleges developed at Vassar and Wells in New York and Bryn Mawr in Pennsylvania.

Great foundations, such as the Rockefeller Foundation, have been set up by wealthy people to provide money for some of the educational institutions and for people's use of them.

Research and the great field of technology took a leading part in education in the Middle Atlantic, because of the tremendous industrial developments. New Jersey for many years has been a center of industrial research, with great technological laboratories associated with her industries and her schools. Pennsylvania has the famous Carnegie Institute of Technology, and there are many other such institutes throughout the region.

No research is more exciting than research in atomic energy—the energy that not only produces the atomic bomb, but that can produce cheap electricity and steam power for peacetime use by the whole world. Early atomic furnaces and stations for generating electricity are at Shippingport, Pennsylvania, at West Milton, New York, and at Brookhaven, New York. These are climaxed by the great plant under construction up the Hudson, to supply power for New York City. You can visit an overlook near Indian Point, on the east bank of the Hudson, and look across at the construction in progress; and you can see exhibits whose parts move to show you how atomic energy can produce electricity.

At Linden, New Jersey, is a big atomic radiation laboratory, where the effects of radiation on people, animals, plants, and materials are studied.

Things to think about

Why is the Middle Atlantic region a region of big cities?

How have the big cities overcome the waters that surround them and adapted them to their needs?

Why do the big cities need the surrounding countryside, its farms, natural resources, and smaller towns?

What things make the Middle Atlantic region such a great center of transportation?

What is meant when this region is called the "great melting pot?"

Why is the Middle Atlantic region the richest and busiest part of our country?

Why is this region the artistic and intellectual center of our country?

Middle atlantic enchantment

Enchantment Made by Men

The earth gives us one kind of enchantment with all of its mountains, oceans and bays, lakes and big rivers and little streams, valleys and canyons and waterfalls, and vast forests. The other kind of enchantment we have made for ourselves.

One place to find this second kind is in our big cities. If we take a look at the biggest city of all, New York, we find an almost unlimited variety of things to see and do, many of them made by man.

Even the many ways into the city are fascinating. Perhaps you arrive by car and travel through one of the several tunnels or across one of the many bridges. You may fly in on a big jet plane, or perhaps you come by boat. You are at once aware of the water that surrounds New York, and the many ways in which New Yorkers have managed to make the parts of their city accessible in spite of it.

Regardless of how you come to New York, you find many ways of getting around the city. Ferries and boat trips take you to the various islands, and around the bay, and up the Hudson River. On one island you see the statue that everyone knows from pictures, from the first grade up—the Statue of Liberty, hallmark of our country. You can climb a stairway inside the statue and walk around the island where it stands. The statue and island are a national monument and belong to the people of the United States. You can visit other islands, too, on these water trips, and see the great New York Harbor with its big ocean liners.

In Manhattan you can visit as many museums as you can find the time for—the Metropolitan Museum of Art, the American Museum of Natural History, the new Guggenheim Museum designed by Frank Lloyd Wright. You can visit Grant's Tomb, and at Jumel Mansion you can see the rooms that were Washington's headquarters in the stirring times of 1776; you can see the room in Fraunces Tavern, near the southern tip of Manhattan, where he said good-by to his officers after the Revolutionary War.

You can visit Times Square, at night in a blaze of light, and walk on down Broadway along the Great White Way, most famous theatrical center in the world. You can stroll along Fifth Avenue and window shop at world-famous stores. You can visit Rockefeller Center and spend days there, at the radio and TV studios of the National Broadcasting Company, or the RCA science exhibition hall, or at Radio City Music Hall, largest indoor theater in the world. You can stroll in Central Park or go to the top of the Empire State Building. You can visit the United Nations and see for yourself how world diplomats attempt to iron out the world's problems.

All this is on Manhattan Island. If you want to see the Yankees play ball, you go to the Bronx, and there, too, you can see the famous Bronx Zoo. If you want to visit Coney Island, you go to Brooklyn, where the Brooklyn Botanic Garden and the Children's Museum are equally interesting. You can visit two great airports at Queens—LaGuardia and New York International airports—and also at Queens you can enjoy the Rockaways Playland beaches. You can swim at Jones Beach State Park on Long Island, and fish off the eastern shores of that island.

You can take a trip up the Hudson River, by boat or by automobile, and see the United States Army cadets march at West Point, or visit the Franklin D. Roosevelt home at Hyde Park; to reach them, you will drive through the long, long Palisades Interstate Park, seeing the Palisades of the Hudson, and along beautiful Storm King Highway.

Other Cities Have Enchantment

Philadelphia, with Independence Hall and the Liberty Bell; Annapolis, with the U. S. Naval Academy; Baltimore, with its fascinating Chesapeake Bay setting; Pittsburgh, with its confluence of great rivers and its tremendous steel furnaces—all these are cities that have their own special enchantment. There are many others like them all over the region—cities that have great museums, theaters, industrial plants that welcome visitors, beautiful parks to take their people out-of-doors. They offer a fascinating variety of the kind of enchantment that man has made.

Enchantment of the Land

The kind of enchantment that comes from the gifts of the earth is spread all over the Middle Atlantic. Start with the ocean, and look at the great beaches all up and down the Atlantic, around the barrier islands, along the bays. On the southern shore of Long Island are some of these great beaches, in Jones Beach State Park and other areas. Beaches extend along the New Jersey Coast and the Delaware and Maryland shores of Delaware and Chesapeake bays. The most famous of them is Atlantic City in New Jersey, home of the Miss America Pageant, and for many years a gathering place for beach lovers all over the East. Maryland's Ocean City is another of these famous resort beaches.

On these shores is all the fun that comes with water—swimming, boating, water-skiing, and all sorts of beach fun. Fishing is here, too, ranging from big sea-going boats for deep-sea fishing, to dropping your hook off a bridge or a river bank.

The coastal plains have woodland recreation, too. In New Jersey's Pine Barrens, for example, is the Wharton Tract, a vast area of 96,000 acres in public park, where woodlands, meadows, and bogs offer hiking, fishing, canoeing, camping, plant study, and other recreation.

Then look at Lakes Ontario and Erie, the Finger Lakes, and all the others from little to big. Look as well at the great rivers—at the St. Lawrence River, for example, where the Thousand Islands spread eastward from Lake Ontario. Here, too, are all kinds of water fun, where thousands of summer and winter homes are built along the banks of river or lake. One of the greatest sources of enchantment of all time is a waterfall—so look at Niagara Falls, where tons of water every minute thunder into Niagara Gorge.

Mountain Enchantment

Called the "Mountain State," West Virginia is, in fact, made up of mountains. They reach close along the winding Ohio River, the state's west boundary, where you can see the great coal and steel barges and other boats riding the river. Here is the Allegheny Plateau, with ridges running in every direction, along with the rivers that flow between them. To the east are the Allegheny Front and the Folded Appalachians, where the general direction of ridges and rivers is from northeast to southwest.

59

These are rugged mountains, some of them high and craggy, most of them covered with a thick growth of deciduous and evergreen forests. Rivers tumble from them in beautiful waterfalls, pause to make blue lakes, and cut through the ridges in lovely forested water gaps. Fine highways through the mountains take people into them, and beautiful state parks provide headquarters for hiking and other out-of-door fun.

What has been done for recreation in the West Virginia mountains has also been done in New York, Pennsylvania, and western Maryland. In New York are the Adirondacks in the north, playgrounds for millions of people, with their forested mountain slopes and wonderful lakes. Chief of these are Lakes George and Champlain; between them is Ausable Chasm, one of the country's most famous gorges.

In southern New York are the Catskills, "Land of Rip Van Winkle," with all kinds of mountain fun on trails and water. There are fine scenic highways, with overlooks over rivers and lakes and mountains, and stops at many interesting historical spots.

In Pennsylvania, as in West Virginia, are the Folded Appalachians in the east and the Allegheny Plateau in the west. Most famous of Pennsylvania mountains are the Poconos in the northeast, where, again, mountain recreation is the keynote of the area. They extend southeast to the Kittatinnies, where the Delaware River cuts the world-famous Delaware Water Gap.

Running northeast-southwest along the very crest of the Appalachians is the famed Appalachian Trail, a foot-trail for hikers that goes from Maine to Georgia. There are shelters with bunks, water, and fireplaces along the way. The hikers carry their own blankets and food.

Monuments and Memorials to Yesterday

Enchantment in the history of our country is preserved in the historic parks, the old mansions, the buildings where early government was developed. Fort McHenry National Monument in Maryland is where, when the United States forces were defending it in the War of 1812, *The Star Spangled Banner* was written by Francis Scott Key. Also in Maryland is Antietam National Battle Site, marking one of the important battles of the War Between the States.

In Pennsylvania there is Gettysburg, where the fields torn by the Battle of Gettysburg are a national military park. Also in Pennsylvania are Independence Hall, Independence National Historical Park, and Old Swedes' Church, in Philadelphia; Hopewell Village, where early iron-making can be seen; Valley Forge State Park, with Washington's headquarters; Fort Pitt Blockhouse in Pittsburgh's Golden Triangle made by the confluence of the Allegheny and Monongahela rivers; and Daniel Boone Homestead, the frontiersman's boyhood home.

As we have seen, Washington and the District of Columbia have dozens of spots of historical interest. One of the most outstanding of these is the House Where Lincoln Died, a national memorial.

Along the Delaware River in Delaware, Pennsylvania, and New Jersey are the relics of early Swedish settlement. Center of these are New Sweden and Wilmington, in Delaware, near where Fort Christina was founded, and where there is today an interesting state park. Zwaanendael House, at Lewes, is a museum to preserve relics of the Dutch settlements. The Hagley Museum near Wilmington preserves the first Du Pont powder mills, as well as other early mills that used water power on the Brandywine.

New Jersey, as the state that Washington's army crossed and recrossed in the Revolution, has many sites of various battles and occupations. Interesting among these are Morristown National Historical Park, Washington's headquarters in New Jersey after his famous crossing of the Delaware; and Trenton Battle Monument, 155-foot monument in Trenton with an observation gallery at the top. The crossing itself is marked by Washington Crossing State Park. Princeton Battlefield State Park marks a battle that raged through the very halls of Princeton University. Thomas A. Edison's life and work in New Jersey are commemorated by the Edison Laboratory National Monument at West Orange, where his machine shop, stock room, and laboratory are preserved; by the Edison Home National Historical Site, preserving "Glenmont"; and by Edison State Park, with a memorial and a museum.

In West Virginia are Harper's Ferry National Monument, scene of John Brown's famous raid; historic Charles Town, with homes of the Washington family; and Wheeling, center of important events from the Revolutionary War onward. Tu-Endie-Wei State Park holds an interesting Indian battlefield, and at Moundsville is one of our largest Indian mounds.

New York is rich in the history of colonization and the Revolutionary War and has many state parks and national memorials. The Vanderbilt National Historical Site in New York City is a mansion preserved intact from the "Gay Nineties." The Statue of Liberty, the Roosevelt home on the Hudson, Grant's Tomb—all of these are national memorials for us to see. The Saratoga National Historical Park marks Burgoyne's surrender, and various parks preserve important forts and other historical features at Ticonderoga and Crown Point, on Lakes George and Champlain, at Fort Niagara near Niagara Falls, and at many other points throughout the state. At Cooperstown, where baseball was developed, is a fine museum filled with the history of our national game.

These are only a few of the historical features of our country that have been kept available for you to enjoy along with the wonderful scenery and recreation of the out-of-door parks—preserved for the everlasting enchantment of all people, down through the ages.

Things to think about

What special enchantment can be found in the great cities of the Middle Atlantic States?

Describe the vast variety of natural enchantment found in this region.

Why are there so many national historical monuments and memorials in the Middle Atlantic States?

What are the special things to see and do that make the Middle Atlantic States outstanding and reflect the greatness of this region and of our country?

The District of Columbia

The District of Columbia is not a state, and no part of the District belongs to any state. The people who live in the District do not vote for a Governor and for Senators and Representatives, as do the people of the states. The heads of their government are appointed by the President of the United States, and are responsible to the Congress. The District is really a municipality, which includes the City of Washington, the City of Georgetown, and the County of Washington.

The District was established on land given by Virginia and Maryland. It lies in a great, shallow bend of the Potomac River, in the "Y" where the Anacostia River joins the Potomac, but overlaps the Anacostia for two miles or more to the southeast. So crowded has the city of Washington become that some of its features, such as the Pentagon and the Arlington National Cemetery, the Washington National Airport and the Dulles International Airport, have spilled over to the Virginia side of the Potomac; these are part of Virginia, although they are closely allied to the activities of Washington.

Plans for the city of Washington were first made around the Capitol, on Capitol Hill, highest point in the city, and that plan has always been carried out in the arrangement of all its streets and buildings. An outstanding feature is The Mall, a green parkway from the Capitol to the Potomac, with the Washington Monument and the Lincoln Memorial centered along it. Another is Pennsylvania Avenue, leading from the Capitol to the most impressive residence in Washington— the White House, home of the President of the United States.

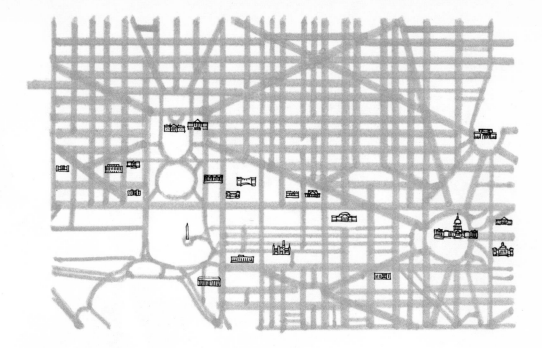

Home of the United States Government

Washington, D. C., home of a great government, is also the home of enchantment. The Capitol Building, high on Capitol Hill, stands first in the land, with its gleaming white marble and towering dome. Inside are magnificent chambers where the laws are made. No building in the world is more impressive or contains a finer collection of art and statuary.

Look west from the steps of the Capitol and you will see two other great structures in line with it—the Washington Monument, a great spire of marble 555 feet tall; and the Lincoln Memorial with its famous giant-sized statue of Abraham Lincoln.

These, with the White House, home of the President of the United States, are the heart of Washington. There are many other interesting places to visit, such as the National Archives Exhibition Hall, where you can see the original Declaration of Independence, Smithsonian Institution and other museums, and the Bureau of Printing and Engraving, where you can see paper money and stamps being printed. The National Wax Museum has lifelike figures of famous people modeled in wax.

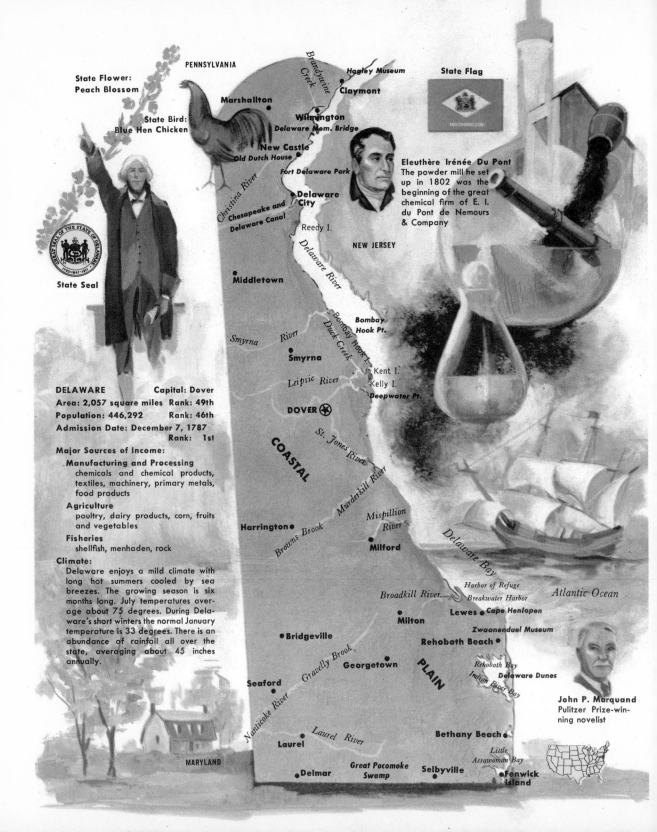

State Flower:
Peach Blossom

State Bird:
Blue Hen Chicken

State Seal

State Flag

PENNSYLVANIA

Brandywine Creek

Hagley Museum

Claymont

Marshallton

Wilmington
Delaware Mem. Bridge

New Castle
Old Dutch House

Christina River

Fort Delaware Park

Delaware City

Chesapeake and Delaware Canal

Reedy I.

NEW JERSEY

Eleuthère Irénée Du Pont
The powder mill he set up in 1802 was the beginning of the great chemical firm of E. I. du Pont de Nemours & Company

Middletown

Smyrna River

Duck Creek

Bombay Hook Pt.

Bombay Hook I.

Smyrna

Kent I.
Kelly I.
Deepwater Pt.

Leipsic River

DOVER ✪

St. Jones River

COASTAL

DELAWARE   **Capital: Dover**
Area: 2,057 square miles   Rank: 49th
Population: 446,292   Rank: 46th
Admission Date: December 7, 1787
                              Rank: 1st

Major Sources of Income:

Manufacturing and Processing
   chemicals and chemical products, textiles, machinery, primary metals, food products

Agriculture
   poultry, dairy products, corn, fruits and vegetables

Fisheries
   shellfish, menhaden, rock

Climate:
   Delaware enjoys a mild climate with long hot summers cooled by sea breezes. The growing season is six months long. July temperatures average about 75 degrees. During Delaware's short winters the normal January temperature is 33 degrees. There is an abundance of rainfall all over the state, averaging about 45 inches annually.

Murderkill River

Harrington

Browns Brook

Mispillion River

Milford

Delaware Bay

Harbor of Refuge

Broadkill River

Breakwater Harbor

Atlantic Ocean

Lewes   Cape Henlopen

Milton

Zwaanendael Museum

Bridgeville

Rehoboth Beach

Gravelly Brook

Georgetown

PLAIN

Rehoboth Bay

Delaware Dunes

Seaford

Indian River Bay

Nanticoke River

John P. Marquand
Pulitzer Prize-winning novelist

Laurel River

Bethany Beach

Laurel

Little Assawoman Bay

Delmar

Great Pocomoke Swamp

Selbyville

Fenwick Island

MARYLAND

Delaware is called "The First State" because it was first to ratify the Constitution of the United States. It is roughly bootshaped, with the back and sole of the boot turned toward Maryland and the front bordered by Delaware Bay and the Atlantic Ocean. Nearly all in the Coastal Plain, the state has in the north a small Piedmont area of rolling uplands. Rivers drain both east and west from slightly raised lands through the central part of the state.

Important Whens and Whats in the Making of Delaware

1609 Henry Hudson discovers the Delaware River.

1631 Dutch settle at Zwaanendael, near Lewes, but are wiped out by Indians the next year.

1638 Swedes establish New Sweden and build Fort Christiana at the present site of Wilmington.

1655 The Dutch take over Swedish settlements and make them part of New Netherland.

1664 The English take over Dutch territory.

1673 The Dutch regain the land but lose it by treaty to England the next year.

1704 From this date the Delaware counties have a separate Assembly.

1776 Delaware declares her independence from England.

1787 Delaware is the first state to ratify the United States Constitution.

We often hear Delaware called the "chemical capital of the world." Here the E. I. du Pont Company has forged ahead in the manufacture of chemicals to provide such materials as nylon, explosives, cellophane, lucite, synthetic rubber, lacquers and enamels, and dozens of other materials in daily use all over the world.

Fine chicken farms head Delaware's agriculture, accounting for more than half of the state's farming income. Other farm products include dairy products, truck crops, fruits of many kinds, hay and grain, and hogs and beef cattle. Canning the fruits and vegetables and processing poultry, pork, and beef are among the major industries of the state.

With so much of Delaware spread along Delaware Bay and the Atlantic Ocean, salt-water fishing is an important occupation. Great quantities of oysters and clams are taken and are shipped fresh to nearby big-city markets and frozen for shipment inland. From many streams, of which the largest is the Nanticoke River in the south, such fish as bass, perch, pike, catfish and trout are caught.

All over the state are reminders of its exciting history. The oldest house in the state is a little Dutch house in New Castle that still stands from one of the earliest settlements. Old Swedes' Church is still in use in Wilmington, and Fort Christina State Park preserves the first permanent white settlement. There are festivals and "days" all over the state when the local citizens, in old-time costume, commemorate its early history, and there are museums and old homes that display the things its pioneers used.

The sometimes marshy eastern shoreline has many fine beaches for water fun, where sailing and swimming are the order of the day; typical of these are the beaches along Rehoboth and Indian River bays. Good highways all over the state take the visitor wherever he wants to go. A gigantic memorial bridge spans the head of Delaware Bay at Wilmington to connect Delaware with the New Jersey Turnpike. There are fine harbors for ship traffic, including those at Wilmington, at the head of the bay, and at Lewes at the bay's mouth.

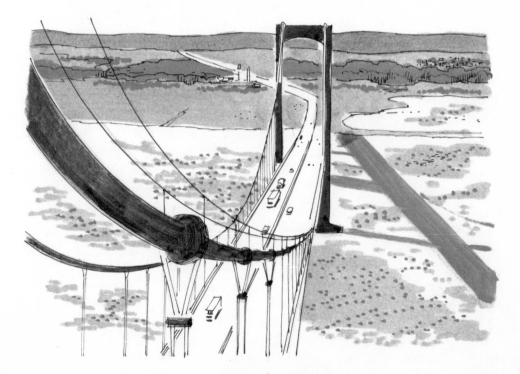

State Seal

State Flag

State Bird:
Baltimore Oriole

State Flower:
Black-eyed Susan

George Herman
"Babe" Ruth
Baltimore-born base-
ball king

John Paul Jones
Naval hero of the
Revolutionary War

Johns Hopkins
Businessman and philan-
thropist; founder of Baltimore's university and hos-
pital that bear his name

PENNSYLVANIA

Cumberland
Backbone Mtn.
Blue Ridge Mountain
Hagerstown
Camp David
Dug Hill Ridge
Mason-Dixon Line
Westminster
Havre de Grace
Aberdeen
Sharpsburg
South Mountain
Parrs Ridge
Susquehanna River
DELMARVA
Frederick
Catoctin Mountain
Towson
Ft. McHenry
Nat'l. Mon.
Chestertown
WEST VIRGINIA
Brunswick
Gaithersburg
Baltimore
Catonsville
Patapsco River
DELAWARE
Wheaton
Greensboro
Silver Spring
College Park
Potomac River
Bethesda
Kent
Island
Denton
Hyattsville
ANNAPOLIS
Easton
DISTRICT OF COLUMBIA
Eastern
Bay
PLAIN
PENINSULA
Patuxent River
Chesapeake
Cambridge
COASTAL
Great Pocomoke
Swamp
Wicomico River
Salisbury
Maryland Pt.
Fishing
Bay
Ocean City
Lexington Park
Princess Ann
Atlantic
Ocean
Potomac River
St. Mary's City
Bay
Pocomoke City
Chincoteague Bay
Pt. Lookout
Tangier Sound
Pocomoke
Sound
VIRGINIA

MARYLAND   Capital: Annapolis
Area: 10,577 square miles   Rank: 42nd
Population: 3,100,689   Rank: 21st
Admission Date: April 28, 1788
                             Rank: 7th

Major Sources of Income:

Manufacturing and Processing
    transportation equipment, chemicals,
    metal products, clothing

Agriculture
    dairy cattle, dairy products, poultry,
    tobacco, truck crops

Minerals
    cement, stone, sand and gravel, coal

Fisheries
    oysters, clams, crabs

Climate:
In the east and south, in Maryland's Coastal
Plain, winters are mild and the summers
are hot; the western section has cold
winters, with snow in the Appalachian and
Piedmont region, and cool summers. The
average January temperature is about
33 degrees and the average July temperature is about 75 degrees. Maryland's
ample rainfall, heavier near Chesapeake
Bay and the ocean, averages about 43
inches annually.

Maryland

Maryland is a state of contrasts. There are three quite different regions in the state—the Appalachian Mountains in the west, the Piedmont through the central portion, and the Coastal Plain in the east. In addition, Chesapeake Bay almost slices the state in two, through the lowest part of the Coastal Plain.

Nowhere on the Atlantic is there a better example of a drowned coastline than Chesapeake Bay, where the mouths of the Susquehanna, the Potomac, and several other rivers have been drowned as the ocean rushed in, forming the bay. Chesapeake Bay is 180 miles long, but its coastline doubles and redoubles in so many inlets and narrow necks of land and twistings and turnings, one on another, that the shoreline is some 3,600 miles long! So here, of course, is a water wonderland, where boating, fishing, swimming, and all kinds of beach fun go on through a long summer season.

Important Whens and Whats in the Making of Maryland

1608-1609	Captain John Smith explores and maps Chesapeake Bay.
1631	A trading post is set up on Kent Island.
1632	Lord Baltimore receives a charter for Maryland from the English king.
1634	The Maryland colony is formally established at St. Mary's on the mainland.
1649	Maryland guarantees religious freedom to all.
1689	Maryland becomes a crown colony, or royal province.
1767	The northern boundary is set by the Mason-Dixon Line.
1788	Maryland ratifies the Constitution of the United States, becoming the seventh state in the Union.

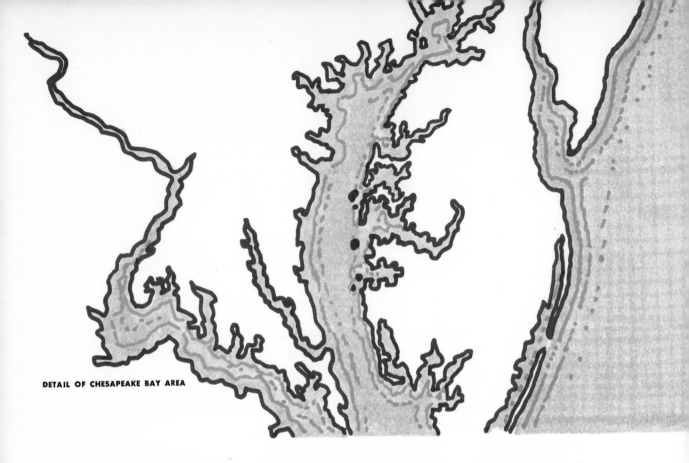

DETAIL OF CHESAPEAKE BAY AREA

The bay is a center for commercial fishing, too, with oysters and clams and hard and soft crabs making up the important catch. To the east the East Shore, or just "the Shore" as it is called by the natives, is the Delmarva Peninsula shared with Delaware and Virginia. Here is a thriving agricultural area, where famous Delmarva chickens hold first place in kinds of food produced. Here, too, as also in the Piedmont, tobacco is grown and dairy products, vegetables, and wheat. Where Maryland reaches the Atlantic, there are woodlands and bay areas where camping and hunting are allowed. Assateague Island, which protects the shore as a barrier island, has wild ponies on it; if you can catch one, you may keep it.

Baltimore is on the wide mouth of the Patapsco River on the west shore of Chesapeake Bay. Maryland's biggest city, Baltimore is one of the country's major seaports, where ocean ships dock for passengers and cargo. Around the harbor there are miles of industrial plants of all kinds; at Sparrow's Point are some of the world's largest shipyards and steel furnaces.

Farther south is Annapolis, home of the United States Naval Academy, where navy ships dock in the fine harbor. To the north the famous Bay Bridge spans more than seven miles across Chesapeake Bay from Kent Island to a narrow neck of mainland formed by two big rivers.

The mountains in western Maryland are in great contrast to the Bay country. The crest of the Appalachians passes from northeast to southwest through the western end of the state, with rugged, forested mountainsides covering many thousands of acres. Typically scenic are "The Narrows," near Cumberland, picturesquely labelled the "Gateway" into the western tip of Maryland, where much of the area is state and national forest properties open for public recreation.

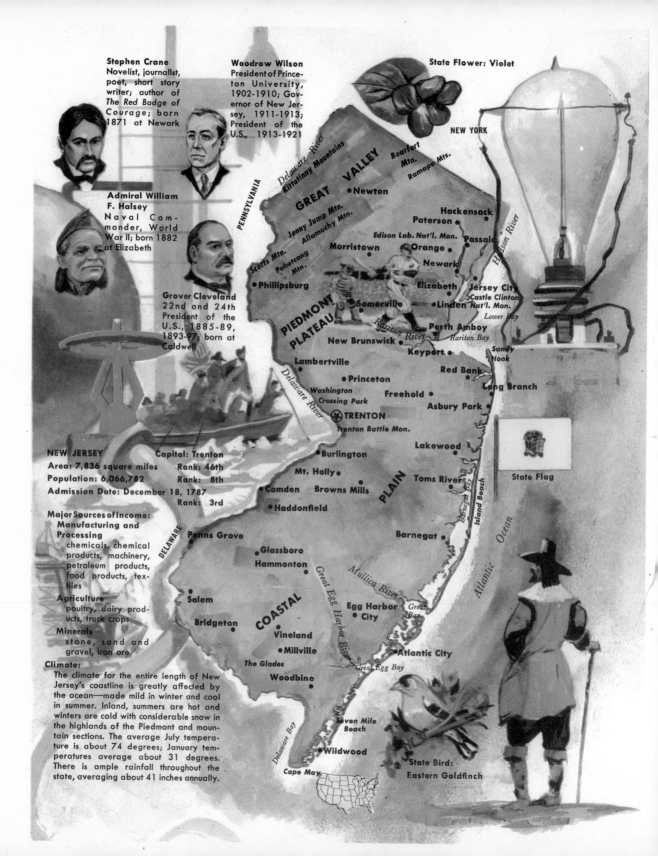

Stephen Crane Novelist, journalist, poet, short story writer; author of *The Red Badge of Courage;* born 1871 at Newark

Woodrow Wilson President of Princeton University, 1902-1910; Governor of New Jersey, 1911-1913; President of the U.S., 1913-1921

State Flower: Violet

NEW YORK

Admiral William F. Halsey Naval Commander, World War II; born 1882 at Elizabeth

Grover Cleveland 22nd and 24th President of the U.S., 1885-89, 1893-97; born at Caldwell

Delaware River

PENNSYLVANIA

Kittatinny Mountains

GREAT VALLEY

Beaufort Mtn.

Ramapo Mts.

• Newton

Jenny Jump Mtn.
Allamuchy Mtn.

Scotts Mtn.

Pohatcong Mtn.

• Phillipsburg

Hackensack

Paterson

Edison Lab. Nat'l. Mon.

Morristown • **Orange** **Passaic**

Newark

Hudson River

PIEDMONT PLATEAU

• Somerville

Elizabeth

Jersey City
Castle Clinton Nat'l. Mon.

Linden

Raritan River

Lower Bay

New Brunswick

Perth Amboy

Raritan Bay

Keyport

Sandy Hook

• Lambertville

Delaware River

• **Princeton**

Red Bank

Washington Crossing Park

Freehold

Long Branch

TRENTON
Trenton Battle Mon.

Asbury Park

Lakewood

State Flag

NEW JERSEY

Area: 7,836 square miles
Population: 6,066,782
Admission Date: December 18, 1787

Capital: Trenton
Rank: 46th
Rank: 8th
Rank: 3rd

Major Sources of Income:
Manufacturing and Processing
   chemicals, chemical products, machinery, petroleum products, food products, textiles

Agriculture
   poultry, dairy products, truck crops

Minerals
   stone, sand and gravel, iron ore

Climate:
The climate for the entire length of New Jersey's coastline is greatly affected by the ocean—made mild in winter and cool in summer. Inland, summers are hot and winters are cold with considerable snow in the highlands of the Piedmont and mountain sections. The average July temperature is about 74 degrees; January temperatures average about 31 degrees. There is ample rainfall throughout the state, averaging about 41 inches annually.

• **Burlington**

Mt. Holly

Toms River

Barnegat Bay

Island Beach

PLAIN

• **Camden** **Browns Mills**

• **Haddonfield**

DELAWARE

Penns Grove

Barnegat

• **Glassboro**
Hammonton

Great Egg Harbor River

Mullica River

Atlantic Ocean

Salem

COASTAL

Egg Harbor City

Great Bay

Bridgeton

Vineland

• **Millville**

The Glades

Woodbine

Atlantic City

Great Egg Bay

Delaware Bay

Seven Mile Beach

• **Wildwood**

Cape May

State Bird: Eastern Goldfinch

Following the pattern of states in the Middle Atlantic, New Jersey is very largely bordered by the waters of her drowned seacoast. To these—the Atlantic Ocean and the deeply-penetrating Delaware Bay —add the long, long line of the Delaware River, and you find that the only boundary of New Jersey on dry land is the one across the narrow northern corridor.

Important Whens and Whats in the Making of New Jersey

1609 A party from Henry Hudson's *Half Moon* explores Newark Bay.

1618-1620 Dutch establish the first settlements near what is now Jersey City.

1640 Swedes settle along the Delaware River.

1655 The Dutch seize Swedish settlements and make them part of New Netherland.

1664 The English take over Dutch colonies.

1702 New Jersey becomes a royal province, or crown colony.

1776 New Jersey declares her independence from England.

1781 American and French troops headed by Washington and Lafayette march across New Jersey to defeat the British and end the Revolutionary War.

1787 New Jersey ratifies the United States Constitution.

Sometimes New Jersey is called the "Industrial Crossroads of the East," because of the great industries that center there. The state is the greatest producer of chemicals, and a leader in the manufacture of machinery, the processing of food, and the manufacture of textiles and clothing. Not only are these goods manufactured in New Jersey, but much research is done here to provide new and better methods of manufacturing, for New Jersey and for neighboring states as well.

New Jersey is situated between two of our biggest cities. On the northeast she borders New York City, and on the southwest, Philadelphia. Life in New Jersey is very much in tune with one city or the other. Hundreds of thousands of people go into them each day to work, returning home at night. Other thousands go in to shop, or to take produce to market, or for fun.

Residents of New Jersey sometimes say that they have a little of everything that exists in America. In the north they have mountains, deeply forested, and many beautiful lakes. In the east they have a fabulous ocean shore, protected by long barrier islands, where beach fun is as fine as can be found anywhere. Toward the south are swampy sections where hunting ducks and geese and other water birds is a leading sport; and there are uplands where the game birds are those like quail and pheasants. All along the shore, and up the drowned inlets and along the rivers and smaller streams, is wonderful fishing, for bluefish and herring, kingfish and mackerel, bass, shad, flounders, and many, many others. Quantities of oysters and clams are taken from the shellfish beds of Delaware Bay, and these fisheries are among the state's most interesting features.

From New Jersey's farms, in the Piedmont uplands and the Coastal Plain, comes a large proportion of the fresh vegetables feeding the people of the great nearby cities. Here, too, are dairy farms, backed up by farms to grow feed for the cattle. And here are thousands of beautiful gardens, with many commercial gardens that grow plants sold all over the world. Roses, especially, are grown commercially in New Jersey, and you can see them covering acres where nothing else is grown.

Millard Fillmore
Thirteenth President, 1850-1853

Martin VanBuren
Eighth President, 1837-1841

CANADA

Franklin D. Roosevelt
Thirty-second President, 1933-1945

Theodore Roosevelt
Twenty-fifth President, 1901-1909

State Bird: Bluebird (unofficial)
State Flower: Rose

State Seal

St. Lawrence River

THOUSAND ISLANDS

Ogdensburg

Malone

LOON LAKE MTS.

Whiteface Mtn.

Lake Placid

Plattsburgh

Lake Champlain

Mt. Marcy

Santanoni Pk.

Adirondack

Fort Ticonderoga

Blue Mtn.

Panther Mtn.

Mountains

VERMONT

Watertown

Lake Ontario

Lake George

MOUNTAINS

Oswego

Rome

Utica

Hamilton Mtn.

Saratoga Springs

Rochester

Syracuse

Oneida Lake

Niagara Falls

Niagara Falls

CANADA

Buffalo

Finger Lakes

Skaneateles Lake

Owasco Lake

Cayuga Lake

Mohawk River

Troy

Schenectady

Taconic Mountains

MASSACHUSETTS

Lake Erie

Fredonia

Canandaigua Lake

Keuka Lake

PLATEAU

Cooperstown

ALBANY

Tug Hill

Chautauqua Lake

Salamanca

Ithaca

Binghamton

APPALACHIAN

Catskill Mountains

Hudson

Jamestown

Olean

Corning

Elmira

ALLEGHENY

Delaware River

Kingston

Shawangunk Mts.

Hudson River

Hyde Park

Poughkeepsie

CONNECTICUT

PENNSYLVANIA

West Point

Long Island Sound

Yonkers

New York

East River

LONG ISLAND

Staten Island

Atlantic Ocean

NEW JERSEY

NEW YORK
Area: 49,576 square miles
Population: 16,782,304
Admission Date: July 26, 1788

Capital: Albany
Rank: 30th
Rank: 1st
Rank: 11th

Major Sources of Income:
Manufacturing and Processing
clothing, furniture, printing and publishing, photographic equipment, scientific instruments
Agriculture
dairy products, fruits and vegetables
Minerals
cement, stone, sand and gravel, salt, iron ore, petroleum, natural gas

Climate:
Along the seacoast, the lake shores and the St. Lawrence River, and in the mountains, New York summers are pleasant, cooled by the nearness of water and mountains. Inland, summers are hot and the growing season is long. Winters are sometimes severe all over the state and there is always winter snow in the mountains. New York is subject to long "heat waves" and "cold waves," when extremes of temperature take over for days at a time. The average January temperature for the state is 23 degrees; the July average is about 70 degrees. New York has abundant rainfall, averaging about 45 inches annually.

State Flag

When you look on a map at the outlines of the state of New York, you see two strange things. First, this state is almost entirely surrounded by water. Lakes Erie and Ontario and the St. Lawrence River make up almost the whole northwest boundary, the longest boundary the state has. Lake Champlain has a long, long shoreline boundary in the northeast. The Delaware River forms many miles of the southwest boundary. New York City and Long Island are bordered by the Hudson and East rivers, by Long Island Sound, by New York Bay, and by the Atlantic Ocean.

Important Whens and Whats in the Making of New York

1524	Italian navigator Verrazano explores the New York Bay area.
1609	Henry Hudson reaches New York harbor and sails upriver as far as the present site of Albany.
1614	The Dutch set up a fur-trading post at Fort Orange.
1623	Permanent settlers come to Fort Orange.
1625	A colony is established at New Amsterdam, on Manhattan Island.
1664	The English, after forcing the Dutch to surrender New Netherland, rename the land New York.
1754-1763	French and Indian War.
1765	The Stamp Act Congress meets in New York City.
1776	New York declares her independence from England.
1788	New York ratifies the United States Constitution, becoming the 11th state in the Union.
1789	In New York City, George Washington is inaugurated as President of the United States.
1825	The Erie Canal is completed.

The second strange thing is that the state is a triangle, or perhaps a funnel, and at the small point of the triangle, the tube of the funnel, packed in close against Connecticut to the north and New Jersey to the south where it has no room at all to grow, is the city of New York. Tiny as it seems on the map, this is one of the greatest metropolitan areas in the world. Within its city limits live almost half of the nearly 17,000,000 people who live in the state of New York.

New York backs up her great industrial cities with farming and dairying. Milk and cheese flow from the farms of the Allegheny Plateau to the city markets. Many kinds of grain crops are grown there, too. Sweet apples and grapes and many other kinds of fruit are grown in New York. Especially in the Long Island area are big truck gardens that provide fresh vegetables for the city dwellers.

Renowned for her cities and her farms, New York has still another claim to fame—the recreation that she offers. All through her mountains, all around the shore of Long Island, all up the Hudson, all through the Thousand Islands country, all along her lake fronts in the Great Lakes, the Finger Lakes, and the lakes of the northern part of the state, are recreational opportunities as fine as anywhere in the country. You can walk a mountain trail, fish a mountain stream, stalk a deer; you can swim, water ski, sail a boat or race a motorboat, in hundreds of lakes. You can drive along fine expressways and scenic highways in every part of the state, where Indians and early settlers once traveled afoot. In winter you can ski, toboggan, skate, and fish through the ice.

81

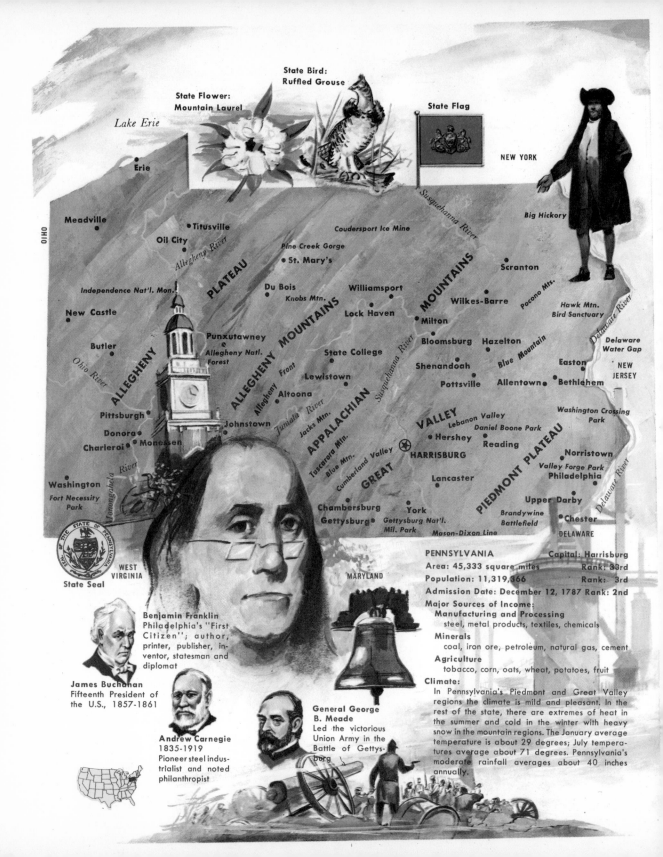

State Bird:
Ruffled Grouse

State Flower:
Mountain Laurel

State Flag

Lake Erie

NEW YORK

OHIO

Erie

Meadville

Titusville

Oil City

Allegheny River

Coudersport Ice Mine

Pine Creek Gorge

St. Mary's

Susquehanna River

Big Hickory

PLATEAU

Du Bois

Knobs Mtn.

Williamsport

Scranton

MOUNTAINS

Wilkes-Barre

Pocono Mts.

Independence Nat'l. Mon.

New Castle

Lock Haven

Milton

Hawk Mtn.
Bird Sanctuary

Delaware River

Butler

Punxutawney

Allegheny Natl.
Forest

ALLEGHENY MOUNTAINS

State College

Bloomsburg

Hazelton

Blue Mountain

Delaware
Water Gap

Easton

NEW
JERSEY

ALLEGHENY

Ohio River

Allegheny Front

Lewistown

Shenandoah

Pottsville

Allentown

Bethlehem

Pittsburgh

Altoona

Juniata River

APPALACHIAN

Susquehanna River

VALLEY

Lebanon Valley

Daniel Boone Park

Washington Crossing
Park

Donora

Johnstown

Jacks Mtn.

Hershey

Reading

Norristown

Charleroi

Monessen

Tuscarora Mtn.

Blue Mtn.

Cumberland Valley

HARRISBURG

Lancaster

PIEDMONT PLATEAU

Valley Forge Park

Philadelphia

Delaware River

Monongahela River

GREAT

Upper Darby

Washington

Fort Necessity
Park

Chambersburg

Gettysburg

York

Gettysburg Nat'l.
Mil. Park

Brandywine
Battlefield

Chester

WEST
VIRGINIA

State Seal

MARYLAND

Mason-Dixon Line

DELAWARE

PENNSYLVANIA   Capital: Harrisburg

Area: 45,333 square miles   Rank: 33rd

Population: 11,319,366   Rank: 3rd

Admission Date: December 12, 1787 Rank: 2nd

Major Sources of Income:

  Manufacturing and Processing
    steel, metal products, textiles, chemicals

  Minerals
    coal, iron ore, petroleum, natural gas, cement

  Agriculture
    tobacco, corn, oats, wheat, potatoes, fruit

Climate:

  In Pennsylvania's Piedmont and Great Valley
  regions the climate is mild and pleasant. In the
  rest of the state, there are extremes of heat in
  the summer and cold in the winter with heavy
  snow in the mountain regions. The January average
  temperature is about 29 degrees; July temperatures average about 71 degrees. Pennsylvania's
  moderate rainfall averages about 40 inches
  annually.

Benjamin Franklin
Philadelphia's "First
Citizen"; author,
printer, publisher, in-
ventor, statesman and
diplomat

James Buchanan
Fifteenth President of
the U.S., 1857-1861

Andrew Carnegie
1835-1919
Pioneer steel indus-
trialist and noted
philanthropist

**General George
B. Meade**
Led the victorious
Union Army in the
Battle of Gettys-
burg

We have only to look at a map of Pennsylvania to see how consistently the mountains and valleys of the southeastern half run from northeast to southwest; and how consistently, in the northwestern half in the Allegheny Plateau country, they run every which way. Cutting through them all are the big rivers, like the Susquehanna. The shape of Pennsylvania is consistent, too—a big rectangle broken by a corridor to Lake Erie in the northwest and the winding line of the Delaware River, which forms the eastern boundary.

Important Whens and Whats in the Making of Pennsylvania

1609	Henry Hudson explores Delaware Bay and the Delaware River.
1638	Swedes establish colonies along the Delaware River.
1655	The Dutch take over Swedish colonies and make them part of New Netherland.
1664	The English take over New Netherland.
1681	England's Charles II grants land, including most of Pennsylvania, to William Penn.
1754-1763	French and Indian War.
1774-1775	The First and Second Continental Congresses meet at Philadelphia.
1776	The Declaration of Independence is signed at Philadelphia.
1777-1778	Washington and his troops winter at Valley Forge.
1787	The Constitutional Convention meets at Philadelphia; Pennsylvania ratifies the Constitution.

Driving through Pennsylvania, however, none of it seems consistent. In the eastern part of the state, the roads follow somewhat the same northeast-to-southwest pattern of the valleys and ridges. You travel beside one mountain range after another, one series of ridges after another running into the next, and you wonder how people ever managed to settle this big, rugged state in the days of the colonies. Sometimes a road cuts through the ridges and you see the layers of the rock exposed —see how crazily they are uptilted and folded on each other, and you wonder what great power was able to push them up and tilt them so. In the western part of the state, too, the ridges are tilted, but here the strata are made up of limestone and sandstone and conglomerate, instead of harder rock; here ridges and valleys and roads, too, run without pattern, in every direction.

Between the ridges and mountains, all over the state, are the fine farms of Pennsylvania. Many years ago people in the cities realized what fun it was to go out to a farm for awhile, and so a special kind of vacation grew up. Many farms let people come and stay for two or three weeks, sharing in the farm life and eating the good farm food, for their vacation.

Driving in western Pennsylvania, you are almost everywhere conscious of this area's coal mining. This is strip mining, where the coal lies just beneath the surface, and you frequently can see the mining going on as you drive by. At many other places you see the dark stain of the prehistoric coal forests and realize that you are in a state where there is much coal in the earth.

You begin to realize, too, the variety of Pennsylvania, with its mountains and valleys, its farms and big cities, its lake shore and great rivers, its mining and its fun.

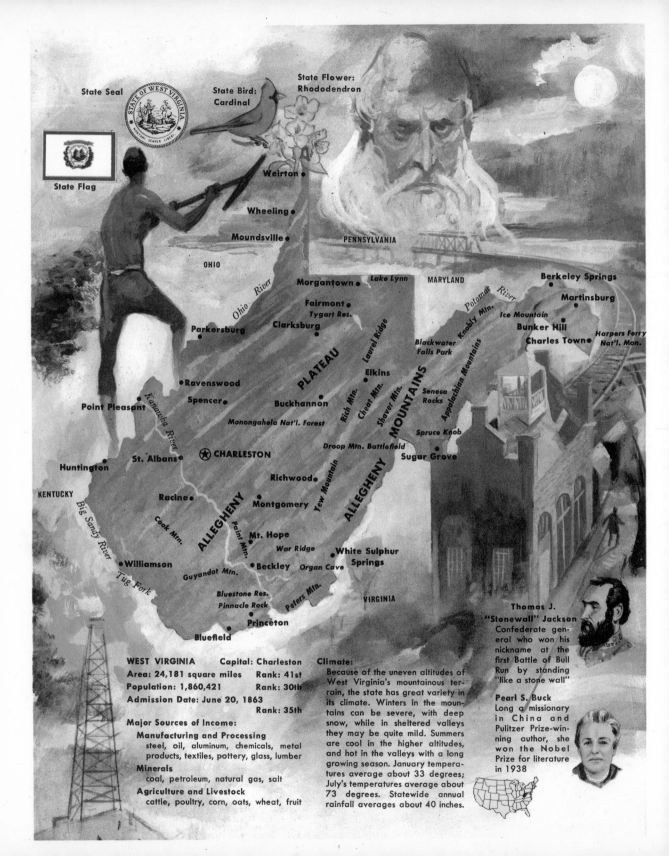

State Seal

State Flag

State Bird: Cardinal

State Flower: Rhododendron

STATE OF WEST VIRGINIA

PENNSYLVANIA

OHIO

Weirton

Wheeling

Moundsville

MARYLAND

Berkeley Springs

Martinsburg

Ohio River

Morgantown

Lake Lynn

Potomac River

Ice Mountain

Knobly Mtn.

Bunker Hill

Charles Town

Harpers Ferry Nat'l. Mon.

Fairmont

Tygart Res.

Clarksburg

Parkersburg

PLATEAU

Laurel Ridge

Blackwater Falls Park

Appalachian Mountains

Ravenswood

Elkins

Spencer

Buckhannon

Rich Mtn.

Cheat Mtn.

Seneca Rocks

Shaver Mtn.

Point Pleasant

Monongahela Nat'l. Forest

MOUNTAINS

Spruce Knob

Kanawha River

Droop Mtn. Battlefield

★ CHARLESTON

Sugar Grove

St. Albans

Richwood

Huntington

Yew Mountain

ALLEGHENY

Racine

Montgomery

KENTUCKY

Cook Mtn.

ALLEGHENY

Big Sandy River

Paint Mtn.

Mt. Hope

War Ridge

White Sulphur Springs

Williamson

Beckley

Organ Cave

Guyandot Mtn.

Tug Fork

Bluestone Res.

Pinnacle Rock

Peters Mtn.

VIRGINIA

Princeton

Bluefield

WEST VIRGINIA   **Capital: Charleston**
Area: 24,181 square miles   Rank: 41st
Population: 1,860,421   Rank: 30th
Admission Date: June 20, 1863
                              Rank: 35th

Major Sources of Income:
  Manufacturing and Processing
    steel, oil, aluminum, chemicals, metal
    products, textiles, pottery, glass, lumber
  Minerals
    coal, petroleum, natural gas, salt
  Agriculture and Livestock
    cattle, poultry, corn, oats, wheat, fruit

Climate:
Because of the uneven altitudes of
West Virginia's mountainous ter-
rain, the state has great variety in
its climate. Winters in the mountains can be severe, with deep
snow, while in sheltered valleys
they may be quite mild. Summers
are cool in the higher altitudes,
and hot in the valleys with a long
growing season. January temperatures average about 33 degrees;
July's temperatures average about
73 degrees. Statewide annual
rainfall averages about 40 inches.

**Thomas J.
"Stonewall" Jackson**
Confederate gen-
eral who won his
nickname at the
first Battle of Bull
Run by standing
"like a stone wall"

Pearl S. Buck
Long a missionary
in China and
Pulitzer Prize-win-
ning author, she
won the Nobel
Prize for literature
in 1938

West Virginia

Even in the Rockies, there is no state more uniformly mountainous than West Virginia. From the border of the eastern "panhandle," where it fronts on the high Blue Ridge, westward through the Shenandoah Valley with its mountain ridges, and still westward through the hills and valleys of the Allegheny Plateau, there is hardly a square mile without its hillsides and a tumbling mountain creek or river. It is said that even the Indians, for the most part, stayed out of West Virginia's mountains because they were so rugged and a hunter could so easily become lost in them.

Important Whens and Whats in the Making of West Virginia

1670-1671 The first exploring parties come to the West Virginia region.

1727 Germans from Pennsylvania settle at Mecklinburg (now Shepherdstown.)

1771 West Virginia begins to demand a separate government from that of Virginia.

1788 Virginia, including West Virginia land, is admitted to the Union.

1818 The National Road is built from Cumberland, Maryland to Wheeling.

1861 At the outbreak of the Civil War, West Virginia counties vote against secession after Virginia joins the Confederacy, and form a separate government.

1863 West Virginia is admitted to the Union as the 35th state.

Today, however, there are fine concrete highways to take mountain visitors and residents alike through the water gaps and along the forested hillsides. Scenic driving, fishing, and hiking can be enjoyed in abundance almost anywhere in the state; in the winter there are skiing, tobogganing, and other winter sports. Fine state parks all over the state are headquarters for visitors.

Rivers run in many directions. In the southern tip, streams running south and those going north to the Ohio have their heads within a mile or two of each other. These are winding, crooked streams, some of them running with the ridges, others cutting through them. Farther north the streams in the eastern part of the state run more regularly southwest to northeast. In the west they run north or west to the Ohio. The Ohio itself, broad and winding, and the Big Sandy running into it from the south, form West Virginia's western boundary.

West Virginia joins her neighbor, Pennsylvania, in the mining of coal and, receiving iron ore by way of the Ohio River and her big cities on the river—Wheeling, Weirton, and others—uses it to manufacture iron and steel. She mines salt brines also, and uses them to manufacture chemicals of many kinds. She drills for oil, and refines it in her industrial cities. So West Virginia, mountainous though she is, is one of the important industrial states of our country.

West Virginia's handcrafts are interesting and are found almost everywhere in the state. Fine pottery, handsome wood-carving and hand-made furniture, corncob dolls, beautiful quilts, and weaving of all kinds are produced all through the mountains and have become famous for their artistry.

89

Glossary

anthracite (ăn′thrȧ sīt) a hard natural coal, of high luster, differing from bituminous coal in containing little airy matter.

arsenal (är′sė năl) a public place for making and storing arms and equipment; hence a storehouse.

bauxite (bôks′īt) an iron substance, consisting of several minerals occurring in some limestone masses and in earthy forms.

bituminous (bĭ tū′mĭ nŭs) a soft natural coal, which yields, when heated, much airy matter.

bog (bŏg) an area filled with decayed moss and other vegetable matter; wet, spongy ground.

brine (brīn) 1. water saturated or full with common salt; 2. the ocean; the water of an ocean, sea, or salt lake.

confluence (kŏn′flŏŏ ĕns) the meeting or junction of two or more streams; also, the place of meeting.

conglomerate (kŏn glŏm′ēr ĭt) rock composed of rounded fragments, ranging from small pebbles to large boulders, in a cement or hardened clay.

craggy (krăg′ĭ) like a steep, rugged rock; full of rough broken cliffs or projecting rocks.

crinoid (krī′noid) one of a large class of marine animals looking and being shaped much like a lily.

deciduous (dė sid′ū ŭs) falling off at maturity, or at certain seasons, as some leaves. Deciduous trees lose their leaves once a year as opposed to evergreens which keep their leaves the entire year, year after year.

emery (ĕm′ēr ĭ) a dark granular, very hard, mineral used especially for grinding.

encroach (ĕn krōch′) 1. to enter gradually into the possessions or rights of another; to trespass; intrude; 2. to advance beyond desirable or normal limits.

escarpment (ĕs kärp′ment) a long, high, steep face of a rock; a long cliff.

famine (făm′ĭn) extreme scarcity of something, as food.

fossil (fŏs′ĭl) any impression or trace of an animal or plant of the past, which has been preserved in the earth's crust.

glacier (glā′shēr) a field or body of ice which moves slowly down a valley from above.

grant (grȧnt) 1. a thing or property given, a tract of land given by the government; 2. a transfer of property, by deed or in writing; 3. to give; to give possession of a title in formal written form.

ground sloth (ground slōth) a slow-moving mammal which stays on the ground, found in tropical forests.

90

horsetail (hôrs'tāl) any of a perennial flowerless plant, related to the ferns.

igneous (ĭg'nė ŭs) resulting from the action of heat within the earth, forming rocks made up of solid masses of minerals.

labyrinth (lăb'ĭ rĭnth) a place full of intricate passageways.

list (lĭst) to tilt or lean; an inclination to one side.

mammoth (măm'ŭth) 1. an elephant no longer living, known by its large teeth and cement-like material between the teeth; 2. referring to size—being very large.

mastodon (măs'tó dŏn) an elephant-like animal, no longer living, differing from a mammoth in the molar teeth.

moraine (mó rān') an accumulation or collection of earth, stones, and debris deposited by a glacier, sometimes being over 600 feet high.

municipality (mū nĭs'ĭ păl'ĭ tĭ) a town, city, or other district having powers of local self-government.

nomadic (nó măd'ĭk) as a group of people, or tribe, that has no fixed location; wandering from place to place.

palisades (păl'ĭ sādz') a line of bold cliffs in a high area or in mountains.

ratify (răt'ĭ fī) to approve and sanction, especially formally; to confirm.

secede (sė sēd') to withdraw from an organization, communion or federation; especially, to withdraw formally from a political or religious body.

sedimentary (sĕd'ĭ mĕn'tȧ rĭ) formed by deposits of sediments, especially particles of rocks transported from their sources and deposited in water.

sinew (sĭn'ū) a tendon; a tough cord.

strata (strā'tȧ; străt'ȧ) beds or layers; sheetlike masses of sedimentary rock or earth of one kind, usually in layers between beds of other kinds.

trilobite (trī'ló bīt) a small marine animal, similar to spiders and most insects, no longer living.

Grateful acknowledgment is made to the following for the helpful information and materials furnished by them used in the preparation of this book:

United States Department of the Interior, National Park Service.

United States Department of Commerce, Bureau of the Census, Field Services, Chicago, Illinois.

Commissioners of the District of Columbia.

Delaware State Development Department.

State of Maryland Department of Economic Development.

State of New Jersey Department of Conservation and Economic Development.

State of New York Department of Commerce.

Commonwealth of Pennsylvania Department of Commerce.

West Virginia Industrial and Publicity Commission.

International Visual Educational Services, Inc., Chicago, Illinois.

Index

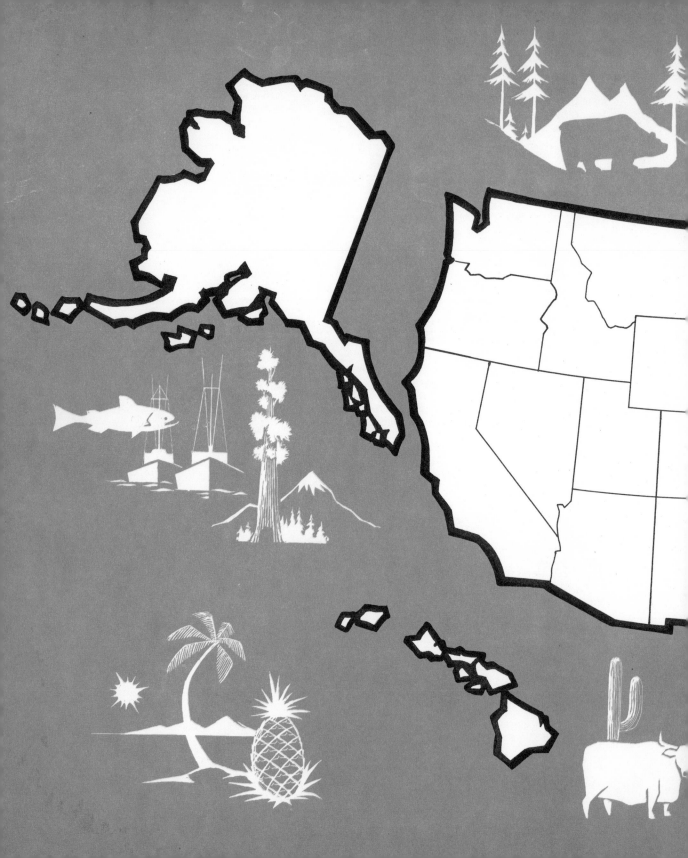